Playing the String Game

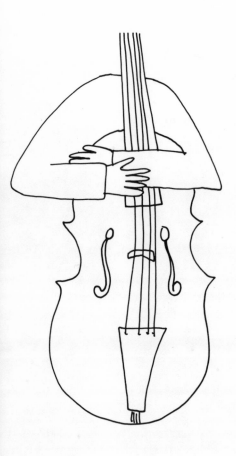

Playing
the
String
Game

Strategies for Teaching
Cello and Strings

By Phyllis Young
Illustrations by Sally Blakemore

University of Texas Press, *Austin and London*

Library of Congress Cataloging in Publication Data
Young, Phyllis, 1925–
    Playing the string game.
        1. Stringed instruments, Bowed—Instruction
and study. I. Title.
MT259.Y69   787'.01'0712   78-7789
ISBN 0-292-73814-5
ISBN 0-292-73815-3 pbk.

Design by Joanna Hill

To Jimmie,

my husband and dearest friend

in the whole world—without whose

support I could never have played the game.

Contents

Acknowledgments

I am deeply indebted to my husband, James M. Young, for the enormous kindness, patience, and encouragement he has shown throughout the writing of this book. I have marveled at his willingness to devote hours to combing the manuscript, and his hundreds of contributions and ideas toward clarifying its contents have been invaluable. Without his help I am sure that the descriptions would have been twice as long and much less clear, if, indeed, the book would have been written at all.

My special gratitude goes to my cello teachers. I believe that this book's emphasis on developing a big, full tone and on covering the entire fingerboard from the start comes from my first teacher, Jeanette Barbour. From Yvonne Tait I learned of the contagiousness of enthusiasm, from Homer Ulrich the importance of knowing the demands made by the entire literature, including symphonic and chamber music. André Navarra's influences are especially felt in my remarks about the love for young people and in parts of Mini-Games 24 and 86.

Ideas stemming from Horace Britt, my teacher for the longest period of time, permeate the book. The references to nature, a positive approach, and the aural concept, plus the ideas expressed in Mini-Games 41, 113, 141, and 151, are rooted in his magnetism. To him all of life, including cello playing and teaching, was truly a game.

From Albert Gillis, the first director of the University of Texas String Project, I learned of the importance of dedication and faith in the student's ability as well as innumerable teaching ideas including those expressed in Mini-Games 79 and 109. I am indebted both to E. William Doty, former dean of the College of Fine Arts on our campus, for having the foresight to support the University of Texas String Project during its growth from a dream in 1948 to a nationally renowned program, and to Charlotte DuBois and Verna Harder for ideas about teaching music to children.

Among my distinguished colleagues at the University of Texas at Austin, I must especially cite George Neikrug. During the four years he taught at our university, I spent many hours observing his incredible ability to teach cello, and I believe this experience dramatically affected my own teaching style. Though he might not identify with them, it is my impression that he influenced parts of at least twenty-seven Mini-Games, including 10, 12, 38, 43, 46, 52, 53, 56, 59, 64, 73, 74, 76, 83, 92, 100, 106, 115, 121, 123, 127, 135, 142, 147, 150, 159, and 164, as well as parts of *The Ready Hand Approach* and *The Great Fall Approach*.

I believe that dinner conversations with my friend and fellow Britt pupil, Margaret Rowell, inspired parts of Mini-Games 20, 70, 90, 101, 103, and 117, as well as *The Rapping Approach*, though she too may not recognize them.

I wish to thank my valued colleague, Stephen Clapp, who teaches violin at our university, for his advice concerning the applicability of each mini-game to the violin and the viola. I also appreciate the interest and encouragement shown by Daniel J. Patrylak, chairman of our Department of Music, throughout this writing project.

As a teacher who tries to learn from everyone and everything, I must express my indebtedness to the American String Teachers Association for its excellent workshops and publications, including the *American String Teacher*. Through this tremendously worthwhile organization, and also at the many lecture-demonstrations sponsored by the University of Texas at Austin, I have had the opportunity to meet hundreds of distinguished string teachers and hear their ideas. Among these are Samuel Applebaum, Robert Klotman, Gabor Rejto, Paul Rolland, and Shinichi Suzuki.

My eternal gratitude goes to my mother and father, who made certain that I had the opportunity and the daily encouragement for music study. From earliest childhood I was aware that originality and creativity were at the top of my mother's priority list. For this influence I am particularly grateful.

And last, but certainly not least, I wish to thank the hundreds of young people I have worked with at the University of Texas at Austin. It has been a privilege to teach my cello students and to supervise the teacher trainees of the University of Texas String Project. The enthusiasm, talent, and dedication of these young musicians have been a continual source of inspiration and joy. The game of teaching cello and strings goes on . . .

Foreword

The purpose of this book is to share pedagogical ideas with the musician who has the good fortune of teaching young people to play a stringed instrument. My hope is that it will help the following: public school teachers seeking new teaching techniques for string classes and for young cello students; private teachers of cello, violin, viola, or string bass on the lookout for fresh, revitalizing approaches to incorporate into their present style of teaching; performing string players with little or no training in teaching or working with young people, either individually or in groups; new, inexperienced string teachers; and university students preparing to enter the string teaching profession.

Creative teaching techniques for cello are emphasized throughout the book. Because of the instrument's size and the position in which it is held, many facets of cello playing are uniquely different from those of violin or viola playing and require vastly different teaching approaches. Yet in some areas the underlying concepts are identical or are so similar that they may easily be adapted to other stringed instruments. I have tried to identify both the distinctions and the similarities.

Though ideally the music teacher is a fine performer on the same instrument as his student and has proven his pedagogical ability, realistically this is not the case in the majority of circumstances. In fact, if all string teaching in our country were restricted to teachers with both qualifications, there would be few string students indeed! Thousands of youngsters would never have the opportunity to realize their dreams of playing these glorious instruments, and vast areas of the United States would be completely barren of school orchestras.

But string teaching is difficult even under the best conditions. We are dealing with an art involving human beings, no two of which are alike. A set of absolute rules that fits all does not exist, and new and unique problems will constantly arise no matter how many years of successful teaching experience one has.

It is my belief that in our art the most challenging aspect of a problem is recognizing that it exists. Many are invisible and inaudible during the early stages of string training and, by the time they have manifested themselves, undesirable habits have already been ingrained. I am further convinced that the formation of good hand, arm, and body positions that prove workable for string playing can best be evolved by sampling the motions required in advanced techniques. Since no tone is produced on a stringed instrument without a physical action on the part of the player, any type of posing, as for a still photo, can prove ineffective in the long run.

The pedagogical device I call the *mini-game* has proven to be priceless in my many years of experience with the teacher trainees and precollege youngsters in the University of Texas String Project. To fulfill a need in meeting various teaching problems as they have arisen, I have devised hundreds of mini-games. For this book 165 have been selected for presentation.

Though cloaked in naïve terms and often taking only a few seconds from the actual music making, these little timesavers, when incorporated with any method or music, can assume the gigantic roles of problem recognizers, predictors, and solvers. In addition, they can be uncannily effective communicators.

The reader may be surprised that throughout the book, even in the technical explanations, I have frequently chosen to use words not traditionally associated with string playing. It has been my experience that students of all ages and teacher trainees respond enthusiastically to the style of language which they consider relevant. My hope is that this unconventional language may fulfill a special need with other string teachers.

Finally, I trust that calling our beautiful profession a game will not shock too many of my colleagues. For years I have observed that, when outstanding string teachers compare their teaching discoveries, their conversation exhibits the zest and enthusiasm of athletes or sports buffs. It is obvious that they love their work and that, in addition to gaining spiritual satisfaction, they derive excitement, challenge, and enormous joy from helping young musicians. To them string teaching is, in truth, a Game.

Playing the String Game

1

The Game

The game of string teaching requires a minimum of two players—the teacher and at least one student. It is traditionally played indoors with the teacher usually standing or sitting opposite the other player(s), who may or may not be seated. The standard equipment consists of an instrument with four strings, a bow, rosin, and music for each player. A music stand, recordings, and cassettes are required or optional depending on the teacher's specifications. Frequently, when multiple participants are involved, the players are equipped with instruments of varying sizes—the violin, viola, cello, and string bass. Considered unseasonal in nature, the game can be played year round, though it is emphasized from late August or early September through May. No standard uniform is required.

Plays

Although the players are not viewed as opponents, the game is comprised of a highly complex system of offensive and defensive actions as well as special strategic moves. The game is further complicated when more than one student is involved, since no player enjoys warming the bench. However, it is generally considered that in the kickoff limited numbers, at least on occasion, can add zest and spirit to the game.

Each play is opened by the teacher.

End Goals

Common end goals are often not shared by the teacher and the student during the first quarter. In fact, a great disparity exists among even the students themselves in the starting lineup and, if one were to learn the true reasons which have motivated youngsters to join the game, the number and variety

would be astonishing.

The goals among teachers are more consistent. Almost universally the string teacher has been motivated to play the game because she loves her subject matter—music, especially as expressed through a stringed instrument; she loves people, especially young people; and she wants to share her love and knowledge of the subject matter with people. The teacher's end goal is to help other human beings learn how to express themselves through music, thereby enriching and coloring their entire lives.

Ground Rules

Five ground rules govern the game:

1. All approaches must be positive and optimistic; any negative comment by a player is considered a foul.

2. Every move made by the teacher is for the good of the student.

3. A mutual respect for each other as intelligent fellow human beings is shown by all players.

4. All players, including the teacher, practice/study at home between lessons.

5. The game should be played in such a manner that it is an enjoyable experience for all participants.

The Teacher

The teacher is a professional whose principal function is to lead the students step by step in the art of string playing in such a manner that each individual play appears relatively simple and flows into the next. Her all-consuming goal is to open the doors of self-expression. Convinced that each person has something within him uniquely beautiful and individual just waiting to be freed, she realizes that she, as the teacher, does

not create it—it already exists. Her role is to guide and help the student develop technical tools so that the internal beauty can flow freely.

The teacher looks on herself as a key holder and recognizes that the ease with which a door is opened has nothing to do with the contents of the room and that untold splendors may lie behind the door with the most stubborn lock. And she believes the medium that her student has chosen for self-expression is one of the most beautiful and elemental of all—the vibrating string.

The teacher overflows with energy. Charged with imagination and creativity, he knows the importance of timing his moves and somehow manages always to capture the moment. He inspires. He looks on each day, each student, and each class or lesson with freshness and zeal, and almost miraculously his boundless enthusiasm lifts both himself and his students above such everyday obstacles as a broken string or noise from an adjacent gymnasium. By the same token, he views the game with great seriousness and realizes, and even hopes, that some of the rookie players may eventually set records surpassing his own. He treasures the individuality of each player and trains no two exactly alike. No student is allowed to be a ditto mark of another and certainly not a duplicate of the mentor; nor is the teacher a copy of any other.

The teacher's appetite for new ideas and thoughts is insatiable. Since he appears to be in a constant state of learning from everyone and everything, including each student at every lesson, one might call him a lifetime learner. And, in view of the fact that love is the basis for all his teaching, he eagerly shares his discoveries, his knowledge, and his skills. He is a giver.

His final goal is to be dispensable.

The Student

Students come in a variety of sizes, ages, colors, and personalities, but they all have one trait in common: they are potentially far more capable than they, and sometimes even their parents, realize.

Following the lead of her mentor, the student's function during the lesson is to discover concepts which it is her duty to apply in home practice. Though she will have many subgoals that sometimes appear non–music oriented, her eventual end goal will be to express the beauty within herself through music and to share it with others.

Duration

The length of the game can vary from thirty minutes to a lifetime, with the players changing from time to time. Eventually the student absorbs the role of the teacher so they become one and, in a sense, he comes to be his own mentor; by the same token, he remains forever the student, with the whole world serving as his teacher.

Scoring

Though there is no official scoring, the game is deemed a success if it stimulates the student's enjoyment of music and if he is able to use it as his profession or avocation should he so desire. Unofficially, points are also tallied by the positive influences of the game on the student's total life, including an increased sensitivity, creativity, effectiveness of study and work habits, persistence, and reverence for life.

Rewards

The game is considered both challenging and inspiring, although such rewards as trophies and plaques are traditionally not associated with it. As thousands have testified, it can give lifetime satisfaction to its participants and can indirectly add enrichment and pleasure to the lives of others.

2 The Starting Game— the Teacher and the Goals

The First Teacher

The teacher of the beginning string student is unique. She must be not only a fine musician and pedagog but also a behavior specialist, a prophet, and an organizer. In addition, if she is a public school string specialist, as are most teachers of beginning string students, she must be a salesperson and a public relations expert. She recognizes that parents, school officials, and students need to be constantly convinced by her and by the success of the string program that the game is worth playing. And, since she herself probably recruited the players, she is keenly aware of the importance of making the game attractive and enjoyable for all.

Because she understands the importance of her work and the special qualifications it requires, she never feels inferior to the master teacher of advanced students. Well aware that such a teacher might easily fumble in the first plays or might fizzle out completely if asked to serve as her substitute, she is cognizant that her own personality and imagination largely determine the success of the starting game.

Primary Long-Range Goals

Always keeping foremost in his mind the ultimate goal of helping the student express herself through music, the first teacher has his own special set of goals and priorities. His primary long-range goals are (1) to establish a solid foundation on which an expressive and facile technique may be built and (2) to keep the student in the game!

After the initial shock and disappointment of having a promising student drop out, the teacher soon learns to develop an intuitive sense for detecting the symptoms that forecast such a move. He uses these as cues for such defensive

plays as the skillful timing of an announcement of a forthcoming program in which the student will perform, the assignment of an exciting new piece, the encouragement for the student to attend a concert by a visiting artist, or simply the showing of a special interest in the student. Aware of the contagious nature of dropping out, he is constantly on guard for signals which predict its possibility and is prepared to take speedy defensive action.

Immediate Goals

In addition to the obvious goals of developing basic musical and technical skills, the first teacher has five immediate goals of the highest priority which serve as guidelines at every lesson and which are of far more consequence than any specific composition that the student will play during the opening quarter. These goals run concomitantly and are interdependent; their total effect on the final score is enormous and, in fact, the absence of any one can cause severe penalties later in the game. Tips for achieving the five immediate goals of the starting game are given in chapter 10.

Immediate Goal 1: To establish the concept of a beautiful tone

This is the single most precious gift the string teacher can give her beginning student. Since the minutes spent in the presence of the teacher are only a fraction of the total time the student will devote to his instrument, his own mental ear must serve as the chief guide throughout all home practice. By taking the role of head coach and manager, the mental ear forms the aural dream of the ultimate ideal to be sought, discerns where the differences lie between the dream and the actual playing, determines which notes or passages need extra work, decides on the ap-

proaches worthy of repetition, and selects the appropriate practice tempos.

If the first teacher makes a special effort not only to insure that his pupil's mental ear is worthy of these responsibilities but also to inspire it to new heights of imagination and sensitivity, study time will be more profitably spent and string playing will be more meaningful to the student. In fact, it is the love for the sonorous, rich tone that can be generated through the instrument and the personal involvement which comes in the attempt to match the external sound with the internal concept that will sustain the student's enthusiasm. The seed to dedication will have been planted.

Imagination is the name of the game.

Immediate Goal 2: To establish the habit of making tension-free motions

The success of the first immediate goal is largely dependent on the teacher's ability to help the student establish the habit of making tension-free motions. No matter how carefully the teacher tries to develop the student's concept of a beautiful tone through the use of live and recorded performances worthy of emulation, the student's mental ear will readily adjust to tolerate the unpleasant sounds produced by tense muscular motions if they dominate her home practice. In the final showdown, the quality of the sounds she hears most often will have the greatest influence on her internal concept of tone. This is particularly true for the more sensitive students.

No tone is emitted from a violin, viola, cello, or string bass unless a string is set in motion, and this can only be initiated by physical action on the part of the player. It must also be recognized that a tone's characteristics reflect the same characteristics of the action that originated it. Thus, if an action is jerky and tense, the tone it produces will also be jerky and tense.

The first teacher realizes the importance of establishing tension-free motions from the beginning lesson and of helping the student discover and remember the feelings associated with them. He knows that such motions will be the student's most priceless possessions and should be guarded and treasured throughout every play; thus, any exercise, étude, or piece which could possibly rob the student of them must be shelved until the habit of producing beautiful tones has been thoroughly established.

Tension-free motion is the name of the game.

Immediate Goal 3: To establish an attitude that is full of confidence and free of inhibitions

As in all enterprises, a major key to success in string playing is confidence in oneself. Lack of inhibition is vital in expressive playing. Therefore, from the very beginning, the first teacher has the unique responsibility and opportunity to establish the attitude of "I can," not "Can I?" Though she is aware that the beginning student has many preconceived attitudes about himself, the first teacher takes advantage of the fact that she is working with new material with respect to performing music.

Confidence is the name of the game.

Immediate Goal 4: To help the student learn how to study and to achieve a sense of accomplishment

While many human emotions—including motivation—can be triggered by other people or incidents, a true sense of accomplishment can come only from a person himself as a result of his own personal endeavor. This is the ingredient that can make even unattractive work interesting.

The teacher understands that both the student and her chauffeuring parent are devoting valuable time to the study of music and that the hours spent in lessons and practice must be well used. Furthermore, he recognizes that, by teaching the student how to practice so the maximum is accomplished during a specific time period, he is helping the student develop transferable skills which will apply to other subjects and will permeate her life style. In fact, these skills will make an enormous contribution toward enriching her life and developing her self-esteem.

Accomplishment is the name of the game.

Immediate Goal 5: To help nurture a love for music and the instrument

The teacher believes that it is love for music and the instrument that is the life-giving force which keeps many people in the game of string playing throughout an entire lifetime. Without this love, there is no possible justification for a human being to devote the necessary hours and energy to study and practice. Although she is cognizant that no

one can make a person love another person, animal, activity, or subject, the teacher realizes that she plays an important role in developing a love for music and allowing it to be expressed freely.

Through experience the teacher has learned to recognize four stages through which many young music students travel. Soon after the *It's fun because it's new* stage, the youngster passes into the *Please the teacher or parent* period. Dominant during the third stage, *It's the thing to do*, is the social aspect of playing a musical instrument and gaining approval from one's peers. Finally the student is swept up into a *Love for playing and identifying with it personally* period which remains with him throughout his life.

Respecting the importance of all four stages in the development of the student as a musician and a human being, the teacher learns to capitalize on them. He also realizes that, since stage four is the only one with truly lasting value, the sooner the student experiences firsthand the energizing force of expressing her innermost feelings and the link between her spirit and her string playing, the stronger her commitment will become. Although this experience is so personal that it is seldom discussed verbally, its presence is evident when one hears the outpouring of personal expression through four simple strings.

The wise teacher learns to detect even a hint or fleeting glimmer of self-expression in the student's playing and strives to draw it out and enhance it.

Love is the name of the game.

3 The Inner and Outer Games

The game of string teaching is composed of two parts: the inner game, which is within the teacher, and the outer game, which forms the communication link between the teacher and the student. With all moves of the outer game being dependent on the inner game, they work together as a team for the good of the student.

The Inner Game

Existing only in the mind of the teacher, the inner game is a silent one. It consists primarily of goals, concepts, motivations, basic principles, and reasons for specific assignments and teaching devices which, if explained to the student in detail at an early stage of his development, would unnecessarily complicate his learning. In fact, burdening him with these inner game processes would most likely hinder and even harm his progress.

Above all, the inner game includes the game plan: a total picture of the growth of a string player, ranging from the first open strings to advanced solo literature. Visualizing the journey her student will take during the years and predicting possible problems en route are by far the most difficult part of the game for the teacher. It is especially challenging if the teacher has never taken that journey herself with the specific instrument concerned, although she may be a fine performing musician on another stringed instrument.

Also included in the inner game are reams of mental notes about the student himself and his experiences. In fact, most students would be astonished to learn how much their music teachers know about them and to what extent this information influences the teaching

methods employed. Unless he compares notes with other students of the same teacher, seldom does a string student have any concept of how tailor-made is his own training.

The inner game belongs exclusively to the teacher. It is, of course, generously shared with young musicians training to be teachers and with those already in the profession. However, the student himself is made aware of it only when and if his teacher deems it beneficial to the learning process.

The inner game determines all moves in the outer game. Only by knowing the motivating factors of the inner games will the teacher be able to make proper and effective use of the mini-games described in the following chapters.

The Outer Game

The outer game, which is the externalization of the inner game, exists in the form of communication with the student.

The string teacher has three primary modes of communication. First, she can speak through her cello or through whatever musical instrument is her specialty, perhaps even using the piano or her singing voice if it has qualities worthy of emulation. Next, she can communicate through physical gestures, including facial expressions. And, finally, she can express herself verbally. All three forms are used by most teachers, at times concomitantly.

The professionally trained musician who teaches a stringed instrument in private lessons or classes, either heterogeneous or homogeneous, generally tends to

rely heavily on the first two modes of communication, since the bulk of his background has dealt with perfecting his own performance skills. Often he has not been made aware of the tremendous power of words and their effect on the behavior of the music student. Though no one would suggest that verbalization can replace the student's seeing and hearing her teacher play, it is believed that resources in this area have remained largely untapped. When combined with the playing and gesturing approaches, exciting new dimensions can be added to the game.

By verbalization, the use of such formidable phrases as the "volar and dorsal movements," the "rotational forces," and the "flexor and extensor muscles of the forearm" is not suggested. Though such esoteric terms might impress the student with the teacher's knowledge, rarely does this type of verbalization have a place in the outer game. Most students would have no idea what their teacher is talking about, and at times he might not either! Even if the explanation is thoroughly correct and understood by all, the danger exists that such focusing on the internal workings of the anatomy might inhibit the natural use of the body.

Except for such simple and inevitable phrases as "try lowering your left elbow," "be sure your thumb is under your second finger," or "not too much ritard," the secret of the verbal approach lies in the teacher's skillful choice of words that trigger the flash of a picture drawn from the student's memory of how something looks, sounds, or feels, which is then related to an instrumental technique.

This is when the tactic called the mini-game enters the field.

4 The Mini-Game Tactic

Almost every physical action required in string playing, when isolated from all others, is similar to one that has been experienced by the student sometime or somewhere in everyday life. Except for very young children, who learn best through imitation anyway, the large majority of students have a vast background of experiences—either firsthand or vicariously through television or the movies.

By calling forth an instant picture or feeling from the enormous storehouse in the brain, the teacher has at her disposal an immense library of practical materials applicable to string pedagogy. Within a few seconds the teacher and the student will have communicated, and music making can be resumed. A bonus is that the student's remembrance of the instructions has been made easier because of the association with something that was already part of himself.

This tactic is called the mini-game.

Its Inner Game

The mini-game can appear deceptively naïve to the rookie teacher if she views only its outer game. Often cloaked in childlike terms, and at times requiring only a momentary interruption in the music making, it modestly conceals an intricate set of inner game mechanisms and strategies understood only by the coach who has spent years in the field working with the total game plan and with many different players.

By relating a specific isolated instrumental technique to an everyday experience, each mini-game has been designed to assist the teacher in one or more of the following ways:

1. To help the student establish a good workable position and approach;

2. To give the student specific checkpoints which are easy to re-

member and use in his home practice;

3. To guide the student in such a manner that she herself will discover a concept, thereby identifying with it;

4. To give the student samples of more advanced techniques which have been reduced to the simplest form in order to insure the future workability of a position or an approach;

5. To detect and remedy a problem which, though quiescent during the first quarter, could manifest itself later and hinder the student's advancement;

6. To help the student remember how his body feels and moves when he executes specific techniques, that is, help him to discover the kinesthetic sense of the action.

7. To help the student discover how to transfer skills and concepts to new material;

8. To help make the music lesson or class an enjoyable experience.

Its Use in Classes

The mini-game is particularly adaptable to a class situation because it gives the teacher an opportunity to check specific aspects of an individual student's position or technique without having to single her out. The entire class can benefit from a mini-game while the teacher, without being too obvious, can observe and help a particular student. The use of mini-games also helps unify the class and contributes to its team spirit.

Its Use with Older Students

The inexperienced teacher or, in fact, any teacher who has never used mini-games may be surprised to learn that many are quite adaptable to the teaching of older students and even adults. Since the student with more years behind

him has had a greater range of experiences and is usually very eager to progress as quickly as possible, he welcomes the comparison of an instrumental technique to anything with which he is already familiar. Obviously the teacher will modify each mini-game to suit the student's age and background and, in the case of the adult beginner, the teacher may find it advantageous to explain some of the inner game processes after the outer game has been successfully completed and transferred back to the music.

Matching the Mini-Game to the Student

The teacher's memory plays an important role in her use of mini-games to good advantage. She must remember which word pictures and images are effective with each student. Since students will have a distinct variety of past experiences and will show their own likes and dislikes, not every student will identify with every mini-game.

When a teacher discovers that a student cannot perform a specific mini-game because he lacks personal identification with the subject matter, it should be shelved immediately. Later, it can be brought out again, either in a different guise for the same student or in the same form for another student.

The Need for Variety

Effective teaching, except for the most exceptional students, requires that the teacher have the ability to say the same thing in many different ways in the outer game, although the inner game objectives remain the same. Thus, a number of the mini-games described in the following chapters have overlapping goals. How often one has heard the exasperated parent or teacher remark: "If I've told him once, I've told him a hundred times." These not uncommon words reveal more about the teaching technique of the speaker than about the learning ability of the student.

For example, if a teacher uses the same words each time she reminds the students that the fingers should be curved, but does not obtain the desired result, the students are not tuned in to her. Just as the drip of a faucet or the hum of an air conditioner, which can be so noticeable during the first two minutes, is soon obliterated by other noises and thoughts, so are ineffective words repeated too often in a music lesson. Recognizing the uncanny ability of the human mind to block out repeated sounds, the teacher needs a large variety of teaching devices. This is where the mini-games can be an effective alternative mode of instruction.

An added advantage of having a wide assortment of approaches is that the chances of the teacher's instruction smacking of a form of nagging are diminished.

Code Words

In the overall game plan the mini-game can prove to be a great time-saver. Not only can it help establish the foundation for a good workable technique, but just the mention of its name can often remind the student of a past lesson. Since the one word or the one short phrase becomes part of a special vocabulary known only to the students and their teacher, it has an elite and secretive quality which is appealing to young people.

Instant Success

Most mini-games will bring about a noticeable improvement in the student's tone and facility almost instantly if the notes are kept extremely simple when the new feeling, position, or action is transferred back to the music. The trick lies in the teacher's skill in gradually adding only one new element at a time to the isolated technique after the successful playing of the mini-game.

The teacher should not be surprised if the technique or position featured in the mini-game is lost by the student in its transferal to the music. This is usually an indication that the process of adding one factor at a time should be slowed down until the new feeling or muscular activity is firmly established.

If the teacher can succeed, however, in transferring this new technique to the music during the lesson so that the student is impressed with the improvement in her own sound, a great motivation for practice will have been formed. The results will have proven that a specific goal is truly attainable and that the establishment of the new habit is worth pursuing.

The commonplace admonition to "practice hours and eventually you will sound better" has no place in the inner-outer game approach. More appropriately the teacher will advise:

Listen to how good you sound when you do it this way. It's important for you to remember the steps we took during the lesson to bring this about so you can repeat them at home. After all, if you can sound like this on two or three notes, you can play four or five just as beautifully, and finally the whole page. Repeat your best notes many times at home until you get the feeling, then gradually add the others, using your inner ear as the guide.

Your goal will be to establish this new feeling or position as a habit and to make it an automatic part of your playing. Since you've done it well several times here in your lesson, you know you can do it at home.

This is not to imply that hours of practice are not required in learning to play a stringed instrument artistically and with ease because, of course, they are. However, the probability of success is increased by placing emphasis on repeating good positions and approaches and discarding undesirable ones.

One hundred and sixty-five mini-games which have proven invaluable in the game of string teaching are described in the following chapters. With a few exceptions, only those concentrating on instrumental techniques and problems are included, since games and devices for general music and music reading are available in other books.

The sentences enclosed by quotation marks are suggested remarks by the teacher. However, it is understood that teachers should feel free to adapt them to their own style of speaking and to the age of their students.

Throughout the book the cello is used as the teaching instrument. Information regarding the mini-game's applicability to the teaching of violin, viola, and string bass is presented under the heading "Team Tactics." Unless indicated otherwise, it is assumed that the string bass students are using French bows.

The mini-games are most effective when interspersed with the assigned music during the class or lesson. *Naturally the music itself must always be placed in the dominant role.*

5 Mini-Games for Better Communication between Players

A true line of communication between the players takes time to build and cannot be forced. Naturally it is the teacher who assumes the lead throughout. Though he appears primarily to be the transmitter, he is also a receiver and at times his students will swear that he must have eyes in the back of his head and an invisible set of antennas picking up silent messages.

In the case of teaching classes of young string players, positive leadership exhibited from the outset is paramount or chaos will result. To clearly establish the procedural rules of the game before a single foul is made is much fairer and is far easier in the long run. The mini-games in this chapter can help the teacher control the class activities and the behavior of the students by letting it be known in advance what is expected. They may be used in any order and may be sprinkled throughout the early months of training as she thinks appropriate.

Monkey See, Monkey Do
Mini-Game 1

Outer Game

The teacher scratches her head, the students mimic her; she points to her right foot, the students do likewise; she touches her left ear, etc.

After gaining the silent attention of the students, the teacher leads them into a specific technique. For example, at the first lesson she can move to a good sitting posture for cello playing.

Then she explains that this mini-game will be played frequently during the course of study for many purposes. She advises the students to listen for the cue "Monkey see, monkey do," which will be the signal for them to observe her closely and imitate her actions.

When to Use

1. At the first lesson.
2. Whenever the teacher desires to gain the concentrated attention of each student's eye.

Inner Game

The teacher knows this is how the student learned to walk, run, and skip. No one taught him verbally how and when to flex his knees! She recognizes that, the sooner her students develop the habit of mimicking motions and take pride in responding quickly, the faster progress will be made. One mental picture of a motion or a posture can be worth an hour's lecture.

This mini-game can serve as an invaluable teaching tool and is especially applicable to class teaching.

Team Tactics

Monkey See, Monkey Do can be played by the entire string class.

Freeze!
Mini-Game 2

Outer Game

When the teacher exclaims "Freeze!" the students know that they are expected to instantly stop moving or playing and to remain perfectly still in their positions. This is a shorter version of "Freeze in your tracks," a phrase familiar to all youngsters.

The teacher explains that this is a helpful teaching device which will be used occasionally throughout the period of study.

When to Use

Anytime the teacher wishes to call attention to a posture—either correct or incorrect.

Inner Game

The teacher is aware that often a beginning student has the impression she must think of a hundred

Mini-Game 2, Freeze!

concomitant things while playing her cello. This mini-game helps by isolating one detail. If the frozen posture is correct, the teacher will cite it as a good example for the student to remember; if it needs improvement, the teacher will guide the student in making the necessary changes.

This sudden cessation of motion is especially useful in teaching a class of beginners. However, care must be taken that it is not used so often that it becomes disruptive to music making.

Team Tactics

Freeze! can also be played by violinists, violists, and bassists.

The Magic Dotted Line
Mini-Game 3

Outer Game

With the tip of his index finger skipping over the student's arm, or whatever part of the body is being emphasized, the teacher says: "Let's check the magic line—dot, dot, dot."

When to Use

When the teacher wishes to stress a particular alignment of the hand and arm.

Inner Game

The teacher knows that the image of an invisible dotted line is not only appealing to a youngster but is also helpful in calling attention to a specific form. If the student's position does not match the magic dotted line, she usually makes an adjustment almost immediately.

This mini-game is most often employed to call attention to the flow of conscious live energy from the body's trunk to the hands making contact with the fingerboard or bow.

Team Tactics

Imaginary dotted lines are helpful in teaching students of any stringed instrument.

Take a Photo, Click!
Mini-Game 4

Outer Game

Continually watching for a good exemplary position, at the appropriate moment the teacher exclaims "Freeze!"

"Quick, take a photo. Click! Remember this position—it is excellent! Note how your _____ looks and feels. Hang on to this photo for your film library."

When to Use

Whenever the teacher spots an excellent position that is obviously working well.

Inner Game

The teacher realizes that the eye is a most remarkable camera and that the brain is a phenomenal film library. By encouraging the student to take mental photos of selected positions, she is helping him build a superb reference library which is readily available for his home study.

The mental film library will consist of three types of photos: (1) still shots taken after the teacher has posed the student or herself; (2) still shots taken when the subject is in motion, similar to the method used by photographers of fashion models, or a single frame clipped from a motion picture film; and (3) motion pictures of exemplary actions. The subjects may be the student himself, other students, or the teacher.

This mini-game is especially useful in class teaching because it encourages the students to learn from each other. Caution should

be taken not to overuse the taking of still photos during the performance of a musical phrase. Also, in the case of certain students, it is advisable to give advance notice that photos will be taken.

Team Tactics

Violin, viola, and string bass students can also improve through mental photography.

Be a Parakeet
Mini-Game 5

Outer Game

Teacher: "Today I want you to be parakeets! When I play a note or a group of notes, listen carefully and try to mimic the sound much like your parakeet learned to talk."

After the students imitate the sounds and are complimented on being remarkable parakeets, the teacher explains:

"Now I'm going to let you in on a secret: all fine musicians have developed the technique for mimicking sounds on their instruments. It can be great fun, and it's challenging.

"We will use this device in most of our lessons to help you learn to play the cello. But you will know that the words 'Be a parakeet' are your cue to listen extra carefully and to be unusually good parakeets."

When to Use

1. In one of the first lessons.
2. Anytime the teacher believes that his own playing or singing will serve as a good model for the student.

Inner Game

The teacher knows that the imitation of sounds is one of the key pedagogical techniques in the early training of music students and that it is the method nature has provided for teaching a child how

Mini-Game 4, *Take a Photo, Click!*

Mini-Game 5, *Be a Parakeet*

to talk. The reference to parakeets is only one of many ways he will encourage the student to imitate sounds.

Though it is fortunate for the student when her teacher is a fine cellist, the piano, the voice, or another stringed instrument can be used effectively. Of course, the teacher never loses sight of his end goal: as she progresses, the student will learn to express herself and her playing will assume more individual characteristics.

Team Tactics

An emphasis on listening, and developing the ability to mimic, aids every music student.

A Secret Signal
Mini-Game 6

Outer Game

The teacher explains that she expects the students to be very alert and to concentrate during the class period but that there will be moments of relaxation triggered by the words "At ease!"

"We need to work out a secret signal which means 'Attention!' Do you have any suggestions?"

When to Use

In the first or second meeting of any instrumental music class which the teacher has not previously taught.

Inner Game

The teacher's goal is to maintain order and discipline in the classroom. She knows that the students will take pride in remembering and responding to the secret signal and that the chances for its effectiveness will be greater if it is thought up by the class itself.

Team Tactics

Signals are important to every member of the instrumental class.

Mini-Game 7, *Skull Practice*

Skull Practice
Mini-Game 7

Outer Game

Teacher: "A fine cellist is like a good champion athlete. She practices and keeps her body in good working order so her muscles are perfectly coordinated as she runs, jumps, and hits targets. Like all good sports participants, she knows the value of skull practice.

"You do this by thinking through an action before you actually perform it. As you hold your body still, you can almost see and feel it move in your imagination. At the same time you can hear the music in your mind's ear! Let's do some skull practice together now so you will know how to use it when I show you a new technique. It will also help you in your home practice."

When to Use

Anytime, but especially when the teacher believes that the student's improvement in performance skills is not commensurate with the amount of time he practices.

Inner Game

The teacher knows that the sooner the student develops the ability to practice mentally the richer the rewards will be. Not only is this a tremendous timesaver, but the student's accuracy will be greatly improved.

Team Tactics

Skull Practice is a must for every instrumentalist.

6 Mini-Games for Posture and Instrument Hold

The form of the string player in action, as in any sport or other physical activity requiring coordinated skill and strength, is vital and can either help or hinder his advancement. Yet how can one explain the disparity of positions of the instruments exhibited by professionals? Even the concert-going layperson can discern obvious differences among the cellists within one symphony orchestra.

By stressing the dominant underlying principles which characterize the approach of most fine cellists, even though it often appears that they have little in common, the following mini-games are designed to help the teacher and the student discover the best position for the individual player. Many of the ideas are transferable to the violin, viola, and string bass, as explained under the heading "Team Tactics." A list of checkpoints for home practice is given at the end of the chapter.

INDIVIDUAL MINI-GAMES

The Elegant Horseback Rider
Mini-Game 8

Outer Game

The teacher gains the concentrated attention of the students by announcing "Monkey see, monkey do" and proceeds to lead them to a good sitting posture for cello playing. As he sits on the front half of his chair, his body will be leaned slightly forward and his feet will be placed apart. He repeats the process with his chair turned sideways to the class so that the students can see the profile of his body.

"Notice, we look like elegant horseback riders on a fox hunt! Our backs are straight, our heads are erect, and our weight is distributed on three points: the balls of our feet and our seat. Take a photo. Click!"

Mini-Game 8, *The Elegant Horseback Rider*

When to Use

1. At the first lesson, followed immediately by Mini-Game 9, *Jack-in-the-Box*, and Mini-Game 10, *Fitting the Cello*.
2. Anytime the teacher thinks a review is needed.

Inner Game

The teacher knows that it is desirable for a cellist's body weight to be both balanced and leaned slightly forward. In addition, he recognizes that a person is less likely to develop lower backaches after long sessions with the cello if the body weight is distributed on three supports. Furthermore, he knows that riding a horse is an appealing image to a youngster.

Team Tactics

Good posture is important for all members of the string class. The string bass students, however, must often lean over their instruments in order to reach notes in the higher registers. Though *The Elegant Horseback Rider* is essentially a cello mini-game, the emphasis on the body weight being balanced on three points also applies to violinists and violists when seated. Besides, how could anyone slump in the presence of such an example?

Jack-in-the-Box
Mini-Game 9

Outer Game

Teacher: "Sit in your chair in such a manner that it will be easy for you to stand up quickly at any moment. Now you will act like a jack-in-the-box. Stand! . . . Sit! . . . Stand! . . . Sit!"

The student will automatically find a good sitting position for playing the cello. Her body will be tilted slightly forward, with its weight balanced on the balls of the feet and the seat. The feet will soon shift to a position so she can rise quickly without moving them.

When to Use

1. At the first lesson, followed immediately by Mini-Game 10, *Fitting the Cello*.
2. Whenever the teacher notices that the student's body appears to be off-balance, slumped or leaned backward, or in a sprawled position.

Inner Game

The teacher knows that this mini-game forces the student to assume the correct balanced position for playing the cello. In fact, it is impossible to stand up quickly if the

Mini-Game 9, *Jack-in-the-Box*

body is slumped or leaned backward or if the legs and feet are sprawled out.

Team Tactics

Jack-in-the-Box is for every member of the string class seated in a chair.

Fitting the Cello
Mini-Game 10

Outer Game

Teacher: "Continue sitting like you did in *Jack-in-the-Box* while I fit the cello to you. Don't move." The teacher then proceeds to place the instrument in the proper position, adjusting the end pin as necessary for each student.

When to Use

1. At the first lesson, immediately after Mini-Game 8, *The Elegant Horseback Rider*, and Mini-Game 9, *Jack-in-the-Box*.
2. Anytime the teacher thinks a review would be beneficial.

Inner Game

The teacher remembers that the axiom "Fit the instrument to the player—not the player to the instrument" can prevent many problems. Although the teacher's mental image of a professional cellist will serve as her chief guide while fitting the cello to the student, the following seven checkpoints are helpful:

1. Is the C string peg somewhat near the left ear? (See Mini-Game 14, *Tickle the Ear*.)
2. Is there some space between the neck of the cello and the student's left shoulder? (See Mini-Game 13, *The Chipmunk*.)
3. Does the fingerboard look like |, not like /, when the teacher faces the student directly? Can the student's left hand reach both ends of the fingerboard with grace and ease? (See Mini-Game 23, *The Skier*.)
4. Does the student appear to be cradling the cello, rather than clamping it with his knees? (See Mini-Game 11, *Cradling the Cello*.)
5. Is the cello turned slightly to the right so that the front on the A string side is exposed to the player?
6. Is the route clear so that the student will be able to bow on the A and C strings? (See Mini-Game 17, *Clearing the Air Corridors*.)
7. Will the student be able to bow without straightening his arm?

Aware that she cannot bombard the student with all the above details at the first lesson, the teacher primarily wants the student to take home a clear mental picture of himself with the cello, a start on a good position, and a feeling of success.

The teacher should not be surprised if the student veers his neck and head to the right while the cello is being fitted to him. This feeling of the need to dodge is commonplace. When this occurs, the teacher simply removes the cello and begins again, making certain that the end pin is to the left of the centerline of the player's body.

If this mini-game gives difficulty, it is possible that the student's cello is not of the appropriate size, and it should be changed if at all possible.

The teacher may wish to introduce Mini-Game 128, *Handle with Care*, at this time.

Team Tactics

Though this is definitely a cello mini-game, the axiom cited in its inner game applies to all stringed instruments.

Cradling the Cello
Mini-Game 11

Outer Game

Teacher: "When you play your cello, it helps to think of it as being cradled gently with your legs. This will keep it stable, yet you will be able to turn it when necessary."

When to Use

1. At the first lesson to help establish a good position and approach.
2. Whenever the student appears to be clamping his cello with his knees, or if it looks unstable.

Inner Game

The teacher recognizes that clamping a cello is an unnecessary waste of energy and that the locking of the knees can restrict the freedom of elbow movement. In addition, many cellists believe that it prevents the cello wood from vibrating as freely as possible.

On the other hand, if a cello feels unstable, the player will tend to grab it with her left hand, a habit detrimental to building a facile and expressive technique. Also, it must be recognized that a moving target is more difficult to hit!

The word "cradle" seems to have a magical effect on most students and helps them achieve the desired balance. This approach also aids the player in turning the cello slightly when playing a lengthy passage on one of the outer strings.

Team Tactics

Time out for all players except cellists.

Hm-m-m
Mini-Game 12

Outer Game

The teacher overlaps his arms on his chest and breathes out a deep sigh—a symbol of great comfort and relaxation. The student imitates him by hugging her cello and sighing audibly. Music making is resumed immediately unless, of course, it is the first lesson.

When to Use

1. In a beginning lesson to help establish a good position.
2. Anytime the teacher perceives one of the following: the stu-

dent's body appears to be off-balance; there is a lack of unity between the player and her instrument; the body is twisted, with one shoulder farther forward than the other; one or both shoulders are elevated; or there is a hint of tension in the student's body.

Inner Game

The teacher knows that this is a relaxed and balanced position. It automatically eliminates any twist in the body, lowers the shoulders to a natural position, and throws the body weight slightly forward, which will help in tone building and preventing tension in the hands and arms.

Also, this gesture gives the student a feeling that her body and her cello are one unit and that the instrument is in no way a foreign object.

Team Tactics

Hm-m-m is for cello and string bass students only.

The Chipmunk
Mini-Game 13

Outer Game

Teacher: "Is there room for a little chipmunk to walk between your shoulder and the neck of your cello?"

Without moving his trunk, the student waves his right hand between the cello neck and his left shoulder to show that there is clearly enough room for the chipmunk.

When to Use

1. In beginning lessons to help establish a good position and to serve as a checkpoint for the student in his home practice.
2. Whenever the teacher notices that the cello neck is too close to the student's left shoulder; the left elbow is folded at an acute angle; or the left shoulder and upper arm are pulled back.

Inner Game

The teacher recognizes the importance of having some space between the cello neck and the student's body. If the instrument is

held too near the player's shoulder, his left elbow will be forced to fold up at such an acute angle that it will feel tight and uncomfortable. Consider, for example, this posture without an instrument. No one would choose to place her left hand on her own left shoulder, or even an inch or two from it, for more than a few seconds!

Since it is the nature of human beings, especially children, to seek comfort, the student will unconsciously swing her left shoulder back in order to widen the angle of her elbow. Although this incorrect position provides instant relief and may not hamper the performance of a simple first position piece without vibrato, the player is twisted and off-balance. Thus, many technical problems will manifest themselves later, particularly those related to shifting and intonation.

When using this faulty posture the player will produce a sound which falls into one of two categories:

1. A weak tone, which results from a restriction in the flow of energy from the body's trunk. (See Mini-Game 62, *Pulling through a Milkshake*.)

2. A harsh tone, which results because the player, in an effort to achieve more volume, will exert the wrong kind of pressure on the

Mini-Game 12, *Hm-m-m*

Mini-Game 13, *The Chipmunk*

bow stick. A more beautiful tone is created by *allowing* the energy to flow *through* the hand from the ultimate source, the trunk.

Unfortunately the very person who conceives of a big tone and is dissatisfied with a weak sound will be the one most likely to be trapped in the second category.

Though the teacher knows that pressure on the bow stick is a necessary ingredient of a big beautiful tone, he recognizes that its source not only affects the tone quality but is invisible to the student. However, the twisted shoulders are highly visible and are much easier to prevent or to correct at an early stage, before the habit has become ingrained.

Also, the teacher is aware that the young student's arm will grow; thus the bend at her elbow will become tighter. If the teacher has not provided enough room for the arm to grow, the student will surely seek relief by pulling back her left shoulder and upper arm.

Team Tactics

This mini-game is for cello students only.

Tickle the Ear
Mini-Game 14

Outer Game

Teacher: "Check to see if the C string peg of your cello is within a few inches of your earlobe. In fact, it might be so close that it tickles."

When to Use

1. In a beginning lesson to help establish a good position and to serve as a checkpoint in home practice.
2. Anytime the teacher observes that the cello is placed either too high or too low in relation to the student's body.

Inner Game

The teacher recognizes that the student needs some tangible checkpoints to use in his home practice. Since the position will vary slightly from individual to individual, the teacher may choose to change the title of this mini-game.

In any event she will take care that the cello is not held too high, thereby forcing the player to raise

his hand and arm unduly in order to play in first position. The teacher is aware of the need for the live weight to flow through the arm and hand so that the fingers seem to sink into the fingerboard. This sensation is more difficult to acquire in the initial stages if the student approaches the fingerboard from below. Instead, if he raises his hand and forearm higher than the fingerboard, then lowers them into the correct position, he can easily acquire the feeling of sinking. Conversely, if the cello is held too low the player's left elbow will feel cramped.

The teacher is particularly aware that a little girl who is bombarded with the remark, "Your instrument is bigger than you are!" even by total strangers on the street is often prone to hold her cello too high because of the appeal of this attention-getting image.

Since it is commonplace to interchange the C and G string pegs, note should be made that this mini-game is intended to refer to the lower of the two pegs on the side of the scroll closest to the player.

Team Tactics

Tickle the Ear is for cello students only.

Look, No Hands!
Mini-Game 15

Outer Game

The teacher stretches his arms straight out at both sides, level with his shoulders, and exclaims: "Look, no hands!"

While sitting with her cello, the student silently mimics the teacher, thereby proving to herself and to him that she does not need her hands to hold the instrument.

When to Use

1. In the first lesson to help establish a good position.
2. Anytime the teacher notes that the student's left hand is supporting the cello; the body is twisted, with the left shoulder pulled back; or the body appears off-balance.

Inner Game

This gesture demonstrates to both the teacher and the student that the instrument is securely supported by the end pin and the student's legs cradling the cello. One needs only to recall some of the acrobatic passages from the major concerti the student will perform in the future to recognize this important concept of a free left hand.

Mini-Game 15, *Look, No Hands!*

Certainly the hand will have enough to do without supporting the cello!

This mini-game has the added advantage of loosening up the arms and chest so the student will feel ready to play.

Team Tactics

Although some professional violinists and violists advocate the help of the left hand in supporting the instrument, it is generally considered advantageous to be able to free the left hand. In playing this mini-game it is recommended that violin and viola students fold their arms across their chests or allow them to hang down, rather than extending them outward. Bassists can follow the plan described in the outer game.

The Rolling Ball
Mini-Game 16

Outer Game

Teacher: "See this little rubber ball I'm placing on your fingerboard near the nut? Let's see if it will roll right down your strings and land on the floor in a direct line with your left ear. Keep looking straight ahead."

If the real or imaginary ball lands to the right of the ear, it will be a signal that the end pin should be moved proportionately to the left so it, too, will be in line with the player's left ear.

When to Use

1. In one of the first lessons to help establish a good placement of the cello.
2. Whenever the teacher observes any one of the following: the student's fingerboard slanting like / instead of appearing | when she looks at the student face to face; the student's head or body veering to his left as though he is dodging the cello; or the student's neck and the cello neck either cramped together or too far apart.

Inner Game

While introducing this mini-game, the teacher is visualizing the long shifts and fast running passages in the advanced cello literature the student will perform in the future.

She knows that these techniques will be extremely difficult if the cello looks like the Leaning Tower of Pisa when she faces the cellist. Were the teacher to pantomime the execution of fast ascending runs up the fingerboard, she would certainly find them unnatural and doubly difficult with the cello in this faulty position. Her fingers and arm would be forced to accommodate to a fingerboard that veered to the right as her hand moved toward the bridge.

Team Tactics

The Rolling Ball is for cello students only.

Clearing the Air Corridors
Mini-Game 17

Outer Game

After the cello is positioned, the teacher places the middle of the bow on the A string, then on the C string.

"We are checking the air corridors that the bow travels to be sure they are clear."

When to Use

1. At one of the first lessons.
2. Anytime it appears that a knee could obstruct the path of the bow.

Inner Game

This mini-game is a means of making sure that the position of the body and the cello allows playing on all four strings. If a knee obstructs bowing on an outer string although the cello appears to be positioned well, the student will probably need to sit closer to the front edge of the chair and pull his feet back, thereby lowering his knees. After learning how to hold the bow, the student can check the air corridors by himself.

While checking the air corridors, the teacher should also make sure that the student does not have to straighten his right arm in order to reach the bow. If so, the cello should be repositioned higher in relation to the player's body.

Team Tactics

All members of the string class should check their air corridors.

Seated violinists and violists may find that they need to adjust the position of their right legs.

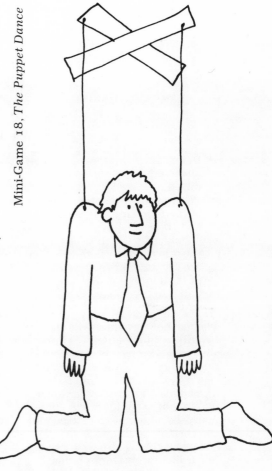

Mini-Game 18, *The Puppet Dance*

The Puppet Dance
Mini-Game 18

Outer Game

Teacher: "Let's have a puppet show. I'll be the puppet master and you be the puppet. First, I'll attach these imaginary strings to your shoulders. Now, when I move them up and down, let's see what happens!"

Sitting with her instrument in playing position, the student jiggles her shoulders up and down while dangling her arms. Every part of her shoulders and arms will bob loosely like a dancing puppet.

"Now let's try the same thing while you pretend you are playing the cello."

The student pantomimes bowing and fingering while her shoulders bob up and down.

Mini-Game 19,
The Parakeet's Toy

When to Use

1. In one of the first lessons when left hand technique is introduced.
2. Whenever the teacher notes one of the following: the student's body is twisted, with one shoulder farther forward than the other; one or both shoulders are elevated; or there is a hint of tension in the student's body.

Inner Game

The teacher recognizes that this imaginary puppet dance is impossible to do if the body is twisted, the shoulders are uneven, or any rigidity exists. When the student immediately returns to her music making, her shoulders will automatically settle into a relaxed and comfortable position.

The teacher is also aware that a fine cellist rarely thinks of his shoulders and body while playing and that his concentration focuses on the music itself and on the impulses in his hand required to achieve his aural dream. However, any hint of rigidity or unnatural position of the shoulders will cut off the power flow from the player's trunk and will handicap her severely. If the beginning teacher assumes the responsibility of making sure that the shoulders are relaxed, the journey the student will travel toward becoming a first-rate cellist will be much smoother.

Team Tactics

The Puppet Dance can be played by all members of the string class. However, with violin and viola students it is advisable to use it as a moment for relaxation without holding the instrument in playing position.

The Parakeet's Toy
Mini-Game 19

Outer Game

Teacher: "Have you ever seen a parakeet's toy that looks like a little penguin? Remember how its weight is distributed so it will immediately bob upright no matter which way the parakeet pushes it? It is beautifully *balanced*. That's the way I want you to be when you play your cello. You will be able to move freely and easily but will always feel *balanced*.

"Let's try it first while standing up over here away from your cellos and chairs. Pretend you are good toy penguins. Glue your feet to the floor. Gently swing left and right; rock your body forward and backward just a little. Let your knees and waist flex slightly when you shift your weight. Look, you can even move your hips and shoulders in a circular motion.

"Now let's sit down in our chairs. Glue yourself to the seat and your feet to the floor. Rock . . . swing and sway . . . move in a small circle. You still make good toy penguins!

"I've never seen a parakeet's toy with a cello, but let's try it. See how your cradled cello moves with you as you gently swing and sway? . . . Now, imagine you're a balanced penguin toy while playing your piece. You will slightly shift your weight here and there but you will always be magically balanced."

When to Use

1. Anytime the teacher feels that calling attention to the meaning and feeling of the word "balance" is appropriate.
2. Whenever the student appears awkward or stiff while playing.

Inner Game

The teacher knows that "balance" is a key word in any kind of string teaching, yet often a student does not identify with the term.

Of course, the teacher will take care that the student does not move her body excessively when she plays. However, this game shows the student how easily her body can adjust to the slightest shift of weight; at the same time, she can feel that the instrument is almost part of herself. The teacher recognizes that the student has constantly balanced her weight in hundreds of everyday activities and wishes to encourage this same natural phenomenon when she is playing her cello.

Team Tactics

The principles and actions described in *The Parakeet's Toy* are applicable to all string instrumentalists.

Cock-a-Doodle-Doo!
Mini-Game 20

Outer Game

The student places his flattened left hand on the top of the fingerboard in about fourth position, with his flattened right hand on top of it. Then he flaps his elbows so he looks like a rooster preparing to crow "Cock-a-doodle-doo!"

Teacher: "Notice how sticky your hands feel. Doesn't it almost seem like they were dipped in wet rubber cement before they made contact with the fingerboard and each other?

"Now let's see if you can discover this same feeling in your four finger pads* when they are lined up on a string in playing position. Flap your left elbow gently until you discover the angle of your arm that seems to make your finger pads the heaviest and the stickiest. Notice how they cling to the fingerboard with each finger feeling flexible and supple. Allow the live weight to flow through! Let's see if you can keep this same sensation while you play your piece."

When to Use

1. In one of the beginning lessons.
2. Whenever the teacher notes that the student does one of the following: seems to be squeezing the cello neck, appears to be pushing down the string with rigid fingers, is twisting his body, or is holding his left elbow unusually low or high.

Inner Game

In the teacher's imagination she is hearing and seeing the beautiful vibrato she hopes will be a dominant characteristic of her student's playing in the future. She recognizes that this is dependent on the combination of strength and flexibility and that one of the surest methods of achieving this desired alliance is through the student's early discovery of the feeling of clinginess in his finger pads while his finger joints, wrist, and elbow feel fluid and free. Once he has discovered this sensation, there is less danger that he will practice at home with his left arm and hand poorly aligned; hopefully, if he should momentarily lose the feeling of clinginess in his hands, he will shift his elbow until it returns.

---

*Throughout this book frequent references are made to the finger pads. It must be noted, however, that the exact portion of the fingers to make contact with the string will depend on the player's hand and the type of passage being performed. In general, cellists tend to use the fleshy part of the fingertips when playing slower passages in the neck positions and the extreme ends of the fingertips for fast passages and in thumb position.

Mini-Game 20, *Cock-a-Doodle-Doo!*

This mini-game has great value when used as a preventive measure. The teacher is well aware that, unless guided carefully, most students will make a valiant effort at pressing the finger hard in order to "push" the string down to the fingerboard. This faulty action tightens the fingers and wrist and the joints can become frozen. If the approach is not remedied before vibrato is introduced, in all probability it will be of the nervous, ugly type.

Should the student have difficulty in discovering this desired clingy feeling when playing *Cock-a-Doodle-Doo!* the teacher should check to be sure that the body weight is leaned slightly forward and that the elbows feel free, as though they are floating. The cello must be positioned in such a manner that the hands feel close to the centerline of the body. Also, the power line from the player's back to his hands should be checked for any form of tension or rigidity that could obstruct the flow of conscious energy.

Team Tactics

This mini-game is designed especially for cello students.

The Giant Floating Magnet
Mini-Game 21

Outer Game

Teacher: "Imagine that there is a giant magnet floating several inches above your head and that you are wearing a weightless steel football helmet. Naturally your head will feel lifted up.

"This really makes you feel like playing!"

When to Use

1. During the first few weeks of lessons.
2. Anytime the teacher notes the student doing one of the following: sitting in a slumped position, sitting hunched over the cello, twisting or leaning her head sideways, ducking her head under, or jerking or bobbing her head.

Inner Game

The teacher recognizes the importance of the person's total body working as a unit in cello playing. Anytime the student's head or body assumes one of the attitudes or positions listed above, her technique will be handicapped.

One needs only to watch the head of an athlete or a dancer and its relationship to his body to gain a better understanding of this basic concept. In the case of cello playing, the player's head should be held in a quiet and balanced attitude so that the freely flowing actions of the arms and hands will not be disturbed.

In addition, the act of stretching up to the giant floating magnet before playing is highly beneficial. If combined with Mini-Game 15, *Look, No Hands!* the student's whole body will feel loosened up and ready for action.

Team Tactics

Imaginary magnets of various sizes are handy tools for the teacher of any stringed instrument. There are many ways they may be used in the adjustment of positions. The string class teacher must remember, however, that at times it is necessary for the bass student to lean over her instrument in order to reach the appropriate place on the fingerboard.

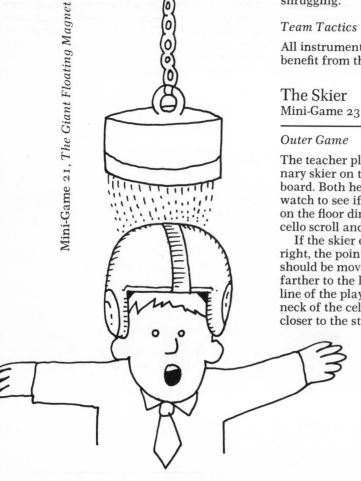

Mini-Game 21, *The Giant Floating Magnet*

The Shrug
Mini-Game 22

Outer Game

Teacher: "When practicing at home, it's a good idea to shrug your shoulders every so often. If it proves difficult for you to shrug them, change your position to make it easy. Let's try it now in both good and bad positions so you can feel the difference."

When to Use

1. Early in the training.
2. Whenever the teacher observes that the student's body is twisted or the student's shoulders are elevated.

Inner Game

The teacher realizes that this common gesture makes a great checkpoint for home practice. When a person sitting in a twisted position tries to shrug his shoulders, he will immediately recognize an unpleasant tightness in his back. Or, if his shoulders are hunched up, he will have to lower them before shrugging.

Team Tactics

All instrumental students can benefit from this simple action.

The Skier
Mini-Game 23

Outer Game

The teacher places a small imaginary skier on the student's fingerboard. Both he and the student watch to see if the skier will land on the floor directly in front of the cello scroll and not to its right.

If the skier ends his jump to the right, the point of the end pin should be moved proportionately farther to the left of the centerline of the player's body and/or the neck of the cello should be placed closer to the student's neck. Care,

of course, will be taken that the cello neck is not uncomfortably close to the person's neck.

"Make your left hand into a friendly fist. Now let it take the role of the skier. However, when it nears the end of the ski slope, instead of landing on the floor, it will return to first position in a circular nonstop motion. Your skier will be making big beautiful loops with smooth flowing motions."

When to Use

1. In the first or second lesson to help establish a good position and a feeling of balance.
2. Anytime the teacher observes one of the following: the student's fingerboard slanting like / instead of appearing | when he looks at the student face to face; the student's head or body veering as though she is dodging the cello; or the student's neck and the cello neck appearing either cramped together or too far apart.

Inner Game

Since this mini-game is an extension of Mini-Game 16, *The Rolling Ball*, the reader should refer to its inner game.

The left hand involvement in *The Skier* helps the student establish a marvelous sensation of balance if her cello is positioned in a good relationship to her body. Should it be difficult for her hand to make a series of continuous loops, the necessary adjustments can quickly be made.

The teacher is aware of the importance of the player's left hand being near the centerline of her body. If the fingerboard is placed far to the left of this line, the hand will feel separated from its power source, the body's trunk. The teacher's observation of a boxer in the ring has made him conscious of this concept and its application to cello playing.

The appropriate location of the fingerboard is quickly established when this mini-game is performed. *The Skier* can even be executed first without the cello, and the instrument can then be fitted to the player so the fingerboard is directly under the skier's path.

In most cases the student will unconsciously turn his wrist slight-

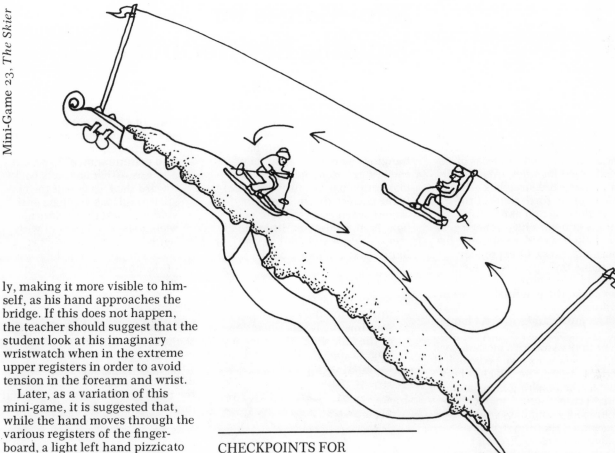

Mini-Game 23, *The Skier*

ly, making it more visible to him-self, as his hand approaches the bridge. If this does not happen, the teacher should suggest that the student look at his imaginary wristwatch when in the extreme upper registers in order to avoid tension in the forearm and wrist.

Later, as a variation of this mini-game, it is suggested that, while the hand moves through the various registers of the finger-board, a light left hand pizzicato be added. All four fingers will pluck the string, working from their springy base knuckles, al-ways returning instantly to the string. If care is taken that the pizzicato is light, that the spring-ing action of the curved fingers is primarily upward, that the side of the thumb clings to two strings in the upper registers, and that the hand remains aligned with the forearm, this variation is an excel-lent means of checking the flow of power from the player's back.

Team Tactics

Although the outer game descrip-tion of *The Skier* is designed for cello students only, the principle of moving the left hand over the entire fingerboard in some manner during the first lessons is applica-ble to all stringed instruments.

CHECKPOINTS FOR HOME PRACTICE

Mini-games, or references to mini-games, may be used as effective checkpoints in home practice. List-ed below are questions concerning the cello student's posture and in-strument hold. Similar lists can be devised for violin, viola, and string bass.

1. Are you sitting like an elegant horseback rider? Is your back straight and your head erect? Is there some weight on the balls of your feet?
2. Could you stand up suddenly like a jack-in-the-box without changing the position of your feet?
3. Can you jiggle your shoulders so you look like a dancing puppet?
4. Is your body balanced so you can rock back and forth like a parakeet's toy penguin?
5. Is the point of your end pin a little to the left of the center-line of your body? When play-ing the role of a skier, can your left hand reach both ends of

the fingerboard with grace and ease?
6. Does your C string peg almost tickle your ear?
7. Is there room for a chipmunk to walk between your left shoulder and the neck of your cello?
8. Do you feel as though you are cradling your cello?
9. Is your cello turned slightly to the right so it is easy to see its front on the A string side?
10. Are the air corridors clear so you can bow on both the A string and the C string? Are your knees out of the way? Can you reach the bow with-out straightening your right arm?

The reader may wish to refer to the following mini-games:
8, *The Elegant Horseback Rider*
9, *Jack-in-the-Box*
18, *The Puppet Dance*
19, *The Parakeet's Toy*
23, *The Skier*
14, *Tickle the Ear*
13, *The Chipmunk*
11, *Cradling the Cello*
17, *Clearing the Air Corridors*

7 Mini-Games for Building Bow Technique

The bow is the magic wand of the string player. With a hank of hair and a stick of wood—from a hollow cavity formed by pieces of wood glued together, over which four strings are stretched—he is able to bring forth some of the most glorious and expressive sounds known. The teacher's goal is to help her student discover the enormous range of expression available through this fantastic tool and learn how to hold and move it so the potentialities seem limitless.

The mini-games in this chapter are intended to serve as a supplement to the student's method book and the teacher's own pedagogical devices. Again, the cello has been used as the teaching instrument, with "Team Tactics" included for violin, viola, and bass students. It is assumed that the string bass students are using French bows. For the most part, the mini-games may be used in any order and are intended to be meshed with the mini-games for building left hand technique presented in chapter 8 and those for varied purposes described in chapter 9. As always, the music itself must play the dominant role throughout every lesson.

The second section of this chapter provides approaches to establishing the cello bow hold by combining mini-games, and examples of checkpoints for home practice are given at the end.

INDIVIDUAL MINI-GAMES

The Dripping Wet Hand
Mini-Game 24

Outer Game

Teacher: "See this imaginary bucket of water? I'd like you to dip your right hand into it. Since we have no towels, I guess you'll have to dry it by shaking off the water. . . .

"Freeze! Look how your hand is hanging! Notice the space between each finger. Remember how this looks and feels because it is exactly the correct spacing for *your* fingers when *you* hold your cello bow. Notice how your little finger seems to grow right out of your hand. Take a photo. Click!"

When to Use

1. At one of the first lessons when introducing the bow hold.
2. Anytime the teacher notes one of the following: the student's fingers appear to be stretched far apart on the bow stick; the student's fingers appear to be squeezed together; the student's fourth finger does not seem to be a continuation of her hand and arm—that is, it juts back toward the frog end of the bow stick and looks angular; or the student's first finger does not seem to be in alignment with her hand and arm—that is, it seems to jut toward the point of the bow like an awkward hook.

Inner Game

The teacher recognizes that when shaking off water the hand automatically falls into the finger spacing most natural for that individual student. In this motion the hand moves as a unit, yet each finger is relaxed and flexible.

Mini-Game 24, The Dripping Wet Hand

The teacher had previously experimented by holding his own right hand in two extreme positions. First, without a bow, he stretched his curved fingers far apart and discovered that they began feeling tense within only a few seconds. Next, he tried placing them close together and observed that they soon began feeling immobile and clamped. He recognized that both positions were unnatural and a great waste of energy. He further discovered that neither produced the best results when he played his cello over a period of time.

The teacher is also aware that, as she progresses to more advanced literature, the student will unconsciously adjust the spacing between her fingers in order to produce the various tone colors conceived by her mental ear. However, the teacher considers this to be a good all-purpose position for the early stages of training.

The reader may wish to refer to "Approaches to Establishing the Bow Hold by Combining Mini-Games" before continuing.

Team Tactics

Shaking imaginary water off the hand before holding the bow is helpful to any beginning string student. However, the fingers of violinists and violists will appear closer together on the bow than those of cellists and bassists, since the placement and angle of the fingers are different.

Two-Handed Bowing
Mini-Game 25

Outer Game

Teacher: "Before I show you how to hold the bow correctly with your right hand, let's hear you bow with two hands! Hold each end of the bow any way you choose, then pull the bow back and forth across the D string so that the hair touches about halfway between the bridge and the fingerboard. Listen carefully—try to find the most beautiful sounds your cello can produce.

"Now let's play on each of the other strings. Watch the string as the bow hair crosses it. See how big you can make the vibrations."

When to Use

1. At the first lesson after learning how to sit and to hold the cello.
2. Whenever the student is not getting the string to vibrate freely while he uses his bow.

Inner Game

The teacher wants the student to discover for himself the tone his cello and bow are capable of producing. Since there is no attempt to teach the bow hold in this mini-game, the student is able to concentrate on the string itself and on getting it to vibrate. Care should be taken that the student's right hand does not hold the bow in any manner resembling the traditional bow hold.

By setting up the goal without presenting rules, the teacher has created a situation in which there is no danger that bad habits will be established. The accomplishments are threefold: first, the student is able to produce good sounds almost immediately; second, he discovers for himself the function of the bow; third, he is establishing a model of a good open string tone which is readily available for his home practice.

Team Tactics

Noncellists can take a breather.

Finding the Balance Point
Mini-Game 26

Outer Game

Teacher: "Every cellist should know exactly how the weight of her bow is distributed. Now, if we were examining a piece of lumber, we would expect the balance point to be in the dead center. Right? But a bow isn't symmetrical and no two are exactly alike. Let's find where yours balances."

The balance point will soon become evident as the teacher and the students place each bow upside-down on the index finger. They will then proceed to learn how to hold the bow at the balance point.

When to Use

1. In one of the beginning lessons when the bow hold is introduced.

2. Before introducing spiccato bowing if the teacher thinks a review is in order.

Inner Game

The teacher knows that in everyday affairs it is far easier and more logical to pick up a long horizontal object at its balance point. In fact, any other approach would seem unnatural. This advantage is not available to a cellist.

By holding the bow at the balance point, the beginning student will find it lighter and more manageable. Also, less strain will be put on the fourth-finger side of the hand. Ideally, the player will feel as though he is holding practically nothing at all, and his hand will remain supple and flexible. After he gains this feeling and has a good start on bowing, the student can gradually slip his hand down to the conventional place on the stick, with some adjustments in weight distribution.

The reader may wish to refer to "Approaches to Establishing the Bow Hold by Combining Mini-Games" at this time.

Team Tactics

This mini-game may be played by all beginning string students.

Pick a Ripe Red Strawberry
Mini-Game 27

Outer Game

Teacher: "See those ripe red strawberries hanging below your hand? Pick some."

As each student picks several imaginary strawberries, the teacher will note that some students are using their first fingers and others their second. She suggests that for this occasion it would help if each person used his second finger and thumb for the strawberry picking.

"Note how sensitive your fingers are. The strawberries feel plump and soft. You're holding them firmly, yet you are careful not to squash them. This is the way a fine cellist feels when she holds her bow. Let's play your piece again with this in mind."

When to Use

1. In one of the first lessons when the bow hold is introduced.

2. Anytime the teacher notes one of the following: the student is squeezing the bow stick and his fingers look tense and hard; the student's second finger is not opposite his thumb; or his thumb is caved in and clamped.

Inner Game

The teacher recognizes that, in the very act of picking the ripe strawberries, the student's hand will shape itself into a gently rounded contour desirable for holding the bow. Also, she knows that the student will instinctively guard against bruising the strawberries. This feeling is easily transferred to the cello bow and will improve the beauty of tone.

The greatest benefit of this mini-game comes from increased sensitivity in the bow hand, which will result in more expressive music. While the human hand has this miraculous inborn quality, the teacher has observed many cases in which a person's manner of approaching the bow appears to desensitize his hand.

Team Tactics

This mental image will trigger the desired physical response with violin, viola, and string bass students as well as those studying the cello. The teacher is advised to vary the object depending on the size of the bow. In many cases raspberries or grapes may prove more suitable.

The Bow Arm's Trusty Aide
Mini-Game 28

Outer Game

Teacher: "When you practice at home, it's a good idea to watch yourself in a mirror. If you see that your right hand has slipped out of a good position while holding the bow, don't try to change it while playing! Instead, stop playing entirely.

"Leave your bow on the string, but let your left hand support the stick someplace in its upper half. Give your right hand a short rest.

"Shake the water off your right hand, let it hang, pick a strawberry with your second finger and thumb, then take a fresh hold on the bow. If the hair makes contact with the string in its upper half near the tip, add one more step after picking the strawberry: tilt your hand slightly to the left so that last drop of water will roll off, then take a fresh hold on the bow.

"No wonder we call the left arm the bow arm's trusty aide!"

When to Use

1. In one of the early lessons in order to help the student establish good practice habits.
2. Anytime the teacher observes a faulty position of the hand or bow and wants the student to make a fresh start.

Inner Game

The teacher knows that it is almost impossible for a player to adjust her hand on the bow from an undesirable position to a desirable one without the help of her left hand. Unless this is explained to the student, she will probably continue to play in a faulty position, thus reinforcing a bad habit.

This mini-game is especially useful in correcting a habit which sometimes crops up among young cellists being taught in a heterogeneous class. Since these students are usually surrounded by violin students, occasionally one has a tendency to adopt the violinist's manner of placing the bow on the string so the stick is farther away from the player than the hair. In correcting this fault, the cello student's wrist will usually fall too low unless he removes his hand, repositions his bow so the stick is directly above the hair or is closer to the player than the hair (depending on his teacher's viewpoint and background), and makes a fresh approach with his right hand.

Team Tactics

The principle of supporting the bow in some manner with the left hand while reestablishing the placement of the right hand on the bow is applicable to all beginning string students.

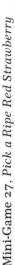

Mini-Game 27, *Pick a Ripe Red Strawberry*

Tracing the Paths of the Bow
Mini-Game 29

Outer Game

Teacher: "Hold the tip of your bow on the D string with your left hand. I'm going to show you how you can trace the path of the bow!"

The teacher checks to be sure that the bow hair is flat, that it makes contact with the string about halfway between the end of the fingerboard and the bridge, and that the bow is parallel to the bridge.

"Dip your right hand in some imaginary olive oil. Shake off the excess. Now smear the oil from your fingers over the top surface of the stick, which will remain stationary. Note that your arm and hand feel fluid and smooth and that your base knuckles are always parallel to the stick. Your first finger, which is leaning slightly toward the stick, is touching it between the first and second joints. Take a moving picture. Remember this bow path, and remember how your arm and hand feel when tracing it. Now let's hear you play some open D's using this path."

This mini-game will be repeated on each string. Mental motion pictures will be made each time, always followed by sound.

When to Use

1. In one of the early lessons after the student has learned the conventional bow hold.
2. When the teacher notes that a review is needed in order to correct the alignment of the student's bow arm and hand or to improve the flowing action of the bow arm.

Inner Game

The teacher knows that this silent mini-game helps the student visualize the actual path her hand should take in drawing the bow. He recognizes that sometimes it is easier for the student to understand an action and to perform and observe it closely if there is silence. Often the tones produced in the class, even her own tones, can be distracting.

The image of spreading olive oil over the top of the stick helps the student discover the concept of a smooth, flowing action of the hand

and arm which, in turn, will produce a smooth, flowing tone. By emphasizing that the oil goes on the *top* surface of the bow stick, the teacher knows that any student who has a tendency to extend her fingers vertically with her base knuckles hovering directly above the stick will unconsciously shift them slightly lower and toward her body; otherwise, the oil would be spread on the bridge side of the stick instead of on the top. This faulty position, of course, is another waste of energy because the weight is applied to the wrong surface. The teacher understands that one essential ingredient of a big tone is pressure of the right kind on the top of the stick so the hair will *sink* into the string, causing it to vibrate.

This mini-game can be effectively combined with Mini-Game 30, *Around the Bend and down a Gentle Slope*. The reader may wish to refer to Mini-Game 60, *The Recipe for a Big Tone*, at this time.

Team Tactics

Violin, viola, and string bass students can trace the bow paths in a modified version of this outer game without using their instruments. The tip of the bow will be held by the left hand as though it has been placed on the string of an invisible instrument.

Around the Bend and down a Gentle Slope
Mini-Game 30

Outer Game

Teacher: "I think of the arm and hand forming a road from the elbow to the bow. When you're playing at the tip, the road is straight and is slanted as though it is on an embankment, but at the frog the wrist has a nice curve and the hand even slopes down to the bow. The road comes around the bend and down a gentle slope!"

After forming the road at the extreme ends of the bow, the teacher guides the students in pulling the bow across the string from one position to the other. She points out that during a downbow, as the elbow gradually moves away from the body, the hand rises to the forearm level, and the thumb becomes straighter. During

the up-bow, as the elbow moves toward the body, the wrist leads so the curve and the slope in the road are gradually restored.

"Hold the tip of the bow on the D string with your left hand. Let's practice forming the road at each extreme end of the bow. Land from above so your fingers touch the top of the bow stick. . . . Now let's hear you play."

When to Use

1. When introducing the whole bow stroke.
2. Anytime the teacher observes that, when playing at the frog, the student does not curve his wrist or his forearm is held too low.

Inner Game

The goal of this mini-game is to help the student form a mental picture of the bow arm at the two extreme positions. Care should be taken that both the upper and the lower parts of the arm move throughout the stroke. This mini-game can be effectively combined with Mini-Game 29, *Tracing the Paths of the Bow*; Mini-Game 4, *Take a Photo, Click!* and Mini-Game 3, *The Magic Dotted Line*.

Team Tactics

This mini-game applies only to the cello. However, the principle of analyzing and describing the shape of the arm and hand when playing in various parts of the bow is appropriate in the teaching of any stringed instrument. The descriptions will vary, of course, depending on the instrument and the length of the player's arm.

The Airplane Stroke
Mini-Game 31

Outer Game

Teacher: "Let's draw some downbows that remind us of airplanes taking off from a runway. As the bow approaches the tip, it will glide up and off so smoothly that the passengers will not realize it has left the ground. . . . Listen to how beautifully the string rings when you do this. Its vibrations keep going on because you've fooled it!"

This mini-game will be repeated on all four strings with successive down-bows, followed by successive up-bows. Later it may be played using shorter airstrips in various parts of the bow.

When successive strokes are played, the airplane should loop around and make another landing on the airstrip without turning off its motors.

When to Use

1. In one of the earliest lessons.
2. In later lessons, repeated frequently.

Inner Game

The airplane stroke is one of the first bow strokes to be learned by young cellists. Its emphasis is on freedom of movement, large motions, and discovery of the joy of the vibrating string.

If used frequently as a warm-up exercise, it will also help the student develop an aural dream of a vibrant tone.

Team Tactics

All members of the string class may play this mini-game. However, many teachers prefer that their beginning violin and viola students delay using the whole bow stroke.

The Railroad Tracks
Mini-Game 32

Outer Game

The teacher slides a bow vertically down a string from the fingerboard toward the bridge so that an ugly scraping sound is produced.

"This is the reason cellists strive to draw the bow at a right angle to the string. Otherwise, this sandpaperlike sound becomes part of the tone.

"Our goal is to draw the bow parallel to the bridge so the tone is golden and pure. Think of a railroad track! The top of the bridge forms one rail and the bow stick the other."

When to Use

Anytime the teacher wants to emphasize the importance of drawing the bow parallel to the bridge.

Inner Game

This mini-game defines the word "parallel" for the young student and helps him understand the importance of this concept.

The teacher recognizes that, later in the training, not every bow stroke should be exactly parallel to the bridge. However, the act of striving to make the bow cross the string at a right angle helps the student gain a good start toward bow control and tone production.

Since the teacher knows the desirability of having many ways of saying the same thing, at another lesson she can point out that the design formed by the string and the bow hair should look like a plus sign, not a multiplication sign.

Team Tactics

Every member of the string class can participate in *The Railroad Tracks*.

Polishing the Furniture and Cleaning the Windows
Mini-Game 33

Outer Game

Teacher: "Hold your bow in the conventional manner. Now let's imagine that you are cleaning house with it! Polish this tabletop and clean those windows and walls!

"Always remember to hold your bow in the conventional manner, although sometimes you will move it in circles and, at other times, up and down or back and forth. Note how your bow virtually feels like part of your body. And, you always have control over its tip."

When to Use

1. At an early lesson when introducing the bow hold.
2. Whenever the teacher thinks this type of activity will improve the student's control and use of the bow. It is especially helpful when he observes that the student is focusing too much attention on her fingers or that the power line between the player's back and her hand appears broken or obstructed.

Inner Game

The teacher recognizes not only that these large motions make the student feel more comfortable with her bow but also that the motions will automatically be initiated nearer the trunk of her body, while her flexible fingers will cling to the bow in a desirably passive manner.

This mini-game can be especially effective if the student places her left hand on her right shoulder blade so she can feel how freely her back muscles are working. Most assuredly her tone will be greatly improved when she resumes playing after the housework is finished!

Team Tactics

Polishing the Furniture and Cleaning the Windows is for all string students.

Mini-Game 34, The Magic Wet Glue

The Magic Wet Glue
Mini-Game 34

Outer Game

Teacher: "See this big kettle of magic wet glue I brought with me today? I'd like each of you to dip your right hand into it."

The students respond and, of course, will discuss the stickiness of the imaginary glue. Undoubtedly their hands will stick to the desk, the chair, the wall, and each other. The teacher may even encourage them to use their left hands to try to free their stuck hands. But, of course, since the glue is magic, this will be almost impossible. Even if they are successful in releasing their right hands by tugging on their arms, they won't go far because of the webs of sticky wet glue.

"Now dip your hand in again, then place it on the bow in a good playing position. Let's hear you play your cello with this wet glue on your hand."

When to Use

1. In one of the first few weeks of lessons.
2. Anytime the teacher perceives one of the following: the student's hand is slipping around on the bow; the student is gripping the bow tightly; the student's fingers appear inflexible; or the student's thumb is tight.

Inner Game

The teacher recognizes the power of the imagination. She knows that with this suggestion the fingers will probably become more sensitive and flexible. If the student has a tendency to grab at the bow, he will discover that this is no longer necessary because of the magic wet glue. This mini-game should bring about a noticeable improvement in the tone.

Team Tactics

The Magic Wet Glue will help all string students.

Comparing the Air Corridors
Mini-Game 35

Outer Game

Teacher: "Let's compare the air corridors the bow travels when you play on each string.

"Elizabeth, place your bow on the C string near the frog as though you are starting a piece with an open C. Donald, you stand near her and set your bow near the frog on her D string. Mary, you place yours on her A string. And Elliott, you set your bow on the G string.

"Look how close your hands are when your bows are at the frog! Your hand certainly doesn't have to move very far when you cross strings. While there is a huge difference in the slant of Elizabeth's and Elliott's hands, they really aren't very far apart. Note how

each hand matches the slant of the bow stick it is holding. See the magic line—dot, dot, dot—I'm tracing with my index finger across the back of Donald's hand. His hand slants the same as his bow.

"Now, remove your bows. This time place them on the same strings near the tip. Wow! What a difference! Look how far apart your hands are! Remember the bow represents the air corridor your hand travels. This means you will really need to think ahead when you change strings at the tip, doesn't it, Gwen? There's no time for surprises!

"Remember that the greater the distance your hand must travel the sooner you have to start preparing for it. And, of course, your arm and elbow levels also change with your hand and bow."

The teacher will lead the student into applying these discoveries to cello playing.

When to Use

1. In an early lesson after the student has learned to hold her bow in the conventional manner.
2. Whenever the teacher notes one of the following: the student is not thinking far enough ahead before changing strings at the tip; the student needs to be more aware of the air corridors the bow travels for each string and their corresponding arm

levels; the slant of the back of the hand does not match that of the bow stick; or a review is in order.

Inner Game

The teacher recognizes that the route the hand and bow travel when bowing on a specific string is only an invisible line in the air which the student must visualize.

This mini-game gives the student something more concrete and brings to her attention the necessity for planning ahead before a string crossing, especially when playing at the tip. It can also help her choose the appropriate part of the bow for specific technical passages.

Team Tactics

Any stringed instrument can be used to compare the air corridors and discover the principles cited in this mini-game.

The Big Full Moon
Mini-Game 36

Outer Game

Teacher: "Let's each draw a big full moon in the air with our right index fingers.

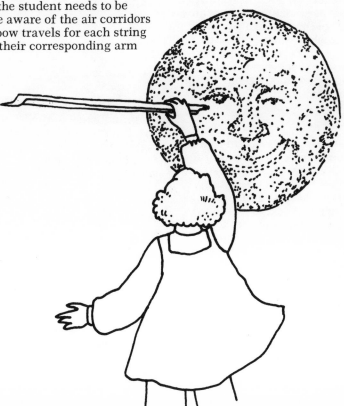

Mini-Game 36, The Big Full Moon

"Now, while holding your bow in the conventional manner, move your hand and arm in the same way you drew the moon."

The teacher continues by demonstrating how to play a succession of down-bow strokes using this circular motion. There will be no interruption in the hand and arm movement when the bow returns to the string, and the string will continue to vibrate even while the bow is in the air. He will call attention to the freely vibrating sound this bow stroke produces as well as the natural pronation of the forearm as the hand and arm move away from the body's trunk when outlining the bottom of the big full moon.

The game will be repeated using a series of up-bows, still following the outline of the full moon, which will gradually become more and more egg-shaped. Finally, the students will play connected down- and up-bows.

When to Use

1. In an early lesson.
2. Anytime the teacher believes that it will help produce a model of a ringing tone for the student to emulate when playing his piece or it will serve as a good warm-up device.
3. Whenever the teacher observes that the student is approaching her bow strokes in a cramped, sluggish manner or the student's bow is not leaning back into the string enough when its upper part makes contact with the string.

Inner Game

The teacher knows that this circular motion frees the actions of the player, thereby causing the string to vibrate freely. The resulting sound should have a ringing quality, which is the basis for a good cello tone. Thus, the very act of playing this mini-game can help the beginning student form the mental concept of a beautiful tone.

The teacher also recognizes the importance of the pronation of the right forearm when the upper part of the bow hair contacts the string—the mental picture of outlining the bottom rim of a full moon will automatically bring this about. Care should be taken that

Mini-Game 37, A Neat Sound Effect—the Tremolo

the imaginary moon is centered directly above the string being played; henceforth only its lower right edge is traced by the hand when the student plays alternating down- and up-bows. Naturally the curve is very slight, and a small ellipse is formed during the change from a down- to up-bow at the tip so that the hand and bow frog are slightly higher at the beginning of the up-bow stroke.

The teacher may prefer for the student to hold his bow at its balance point when this bow stroke is introduced.

Team Tactics

This mini-game is applicable to all stringed instruments. However, many string teachers prefer that their beginning violin and viola students postpone using the whole bow.

A Neat Sound Effect—the Tremolo
Mini-Game 37

Outer Game

"See this imaginary string of little round bells I'm tying along your bow stick? Now shake your hand sideways so you can play some very fast down- and up-bows only two or three inches long. Play at

the tip with flat hair, and let your upper arm move like jelly. Keep the bells jingling! This bowing is called tremolo!"

The students are encouraged to explore all the possible sound effects they can produce by playing tremolo in various parts of the bow. Then they review an old piece with this new bowing.

When to Use

Soon after the student can play a few simple pieces or a piece with several variations.

Inner Game

Though the teacher introduces this type of bowing with emphasis on its sound-effect possibilities, she is actually testing the future workability of the student's present bow hold to make sure it will allow him to play fast détaché and sautillé bowing. If the student has difficulty producing an effective tremolo at the tip, he should lighten the weight on the fourth-finger side of his hand so it is almost released from the bow stick. The elbow should feel as though it is floating and the wrist must be very loose.

Team Tactics

All members of the string class can play this mini-game.

The Magic Tool for Picking up Objects
Mini-Game 38

Outer Game

The teacher asks the student to pick up a number of fairly small objects which are lying on a desk or a table. These may include items some two or three inches wide such as a water tumbler or a blackboard eraser. It is important that the student do this while standing so that her hand will approach the items from above.

At the appropriate moment the teacher will call attention to the fact that the student is relying primarily on her second finger and thumb for this task and that they form the magic tool for picking up objects. Thus, the working hand is naturally balanced so this human tool feels like it is in the center of the hand. He also notes that the thumb is not tight or caved in.

When this sensation is carried over to string playing, the student will find that her bowing is greatly improved.

When to Use

1. At an early lesson when introducing the bow hold.
2. Whenever the teacher notices one of the following: the balance of the student's hand does not appear to be centered at the second finger and thumb; the first finger is hooked under the stick; or the thumb is tight or caved in.

Inner Game

The teacher knows that in almost all everyday activities the student

uses her thumb and second finger as the main tool for picking up small objects. He has consciously observed the action of his own dominant hand throughout the day. Though aware that the total hand works as a unit and that other fingers are also involved, he considers that the prime responsibility of holding objects lies with the interaction between the second finger and the thumb.

When the student is made conscious of this natural phenomenon, she will adjust her bow hold so that her picking-up tool feels as though it is in the center of her hand. This mini-game will help convince her that there is no need for her first finger to hold, lift, and guide the bow; thus, it should not be hooked around the bow stick. Relieved of this unnecessary role, her first finger will feel very sensitive and free. It will then be able to assume other vital functions in the transferring of conscious live energy from the trunk through the hand and arm to the bow stick. The music will come to life.

Team Tactics

This mini-game is applicable to all bowed instruments.

The Ballet Dancer
Mini-Game 39

Outer Game

Teacher: "A beautiful legato bow arm often reminds me of a ballet dancer. Every motion seems to glide through the air like colorful silk ribbons. Even the elbow floats as it goes in and out while playing on one string and up and down when crossing strings. Every movement is liquid."

When to Use

1. Early in the game.
2. Anytime the teacher believes it will help the flowing action of the bow arm.

Inner Game

The teacher's goal is to help the student form a mental image of the dancer's grace which will inspire him in home practice.

Mini-Game 39, *The Ballet Dancer*

Team Tactics

The Ballet Dancer is for all members of the string class.

Zip!
Mini-Game 40

Outer Game

Teacher: "Set your bow on the string near the frog. Notice the contact point between the bow hair and the string. Remember its distance from the bridge.

"Now, we are going to ZIP the bow as fast as we can from the frog to the tip—just barely above the string.' Then we'll stop it on the string at the tip and look again at the contact point. Go!"

The students ZIP.

"Is the bow hair exactly the same distance from the bridge as when your bow was at the frog? Let's try it again and arrive at exactly the same spot!"

After accomplishing this they will practice zipping from the tip to the frog. Repeat in both directions on all strings until the motion is as direct as possible.

Then, the teacher will lead the students back to playing open strings or simple music.

Mini-Game 38,
The Magic Tool for Picking up Objects

When to Use

Anytime after the student has a good start on bowing. It is especially useful when the teacher notes one of the following:

1. The student's bowing is not parallel to the bridge.
2. The student is moving her bow slowly and somewhat gingerly as though she is having to concentrate on it all the time.
3. The student's right arm and hand are not in good alignment when she plays at the tip of the bow; that is, her wrist has gone farther to the right than her hand, causing a detour and obstruction in the power line from her back.

Inner Game

The teacher knows that very slow motions can give a student many opportunities to get into strange positions which can obstruct or misdirect the power flow. In most cases when a person is asked to move as fast as possible from one point to another, she unconsciously takes the most direct route, which is usually the best. A single super-fast motion followed by a stop can often solve many problems.

Team Tactics

Zip! is applicable to all stringed instruments. However, the teacher may prefer that violin and viola students not play it as soon as those studying cello and bass.

Watch the Vibrations!
Mini-Game 41

Outer Game

The teacher asks the students to play some notes or a passage pizzicato, striving to achieve a clear bell-like tone.

"Watch the string vibrate! See how big and free you can make these vibrations.

"Now play the same notes with your bow sinking into the string. Watch carefully to see if you can convince the string to vibrate just as much. Make it ring like a bell!"

When to Use

Whenever the teacher wishes to emphasize the visual and aural effect of the freely vibrating string,

which is the basis for good tone production.

Inner Game

The teacher recognizes that the emphasis on watching a string vibrate can make a vivid impression on some youngsters, thereby helping them gain the total concept—both visual and aural—of the freely vibrating string.

This mini-game is especially effective when played under fluorescent lights. Later it can be extended to include watching the sympathetic vibrations of the other strings.

Team Tactics

Watch the Vibrations! is for the entire string class.

The Sparrow Ride
Mini-Game 42

Outer Game

Teacher: "With your left hand helping, hold the bow out in front of you with a perfect bow hold. Keep the stick as parallel to the floor as possible, at about the height of your shirttail. Remove your left hand, but keep the bow level.

"Look! Four little sparrows are flying in and perching on your bow. They think it's a telephone wire!

"Let's give them a very slow ride up and down as though they are in an elevator. Both ends of the bow will need to stay level or they will become frightened and fly off. Keep

Mini-Game 42, *The Sparrow Ride*

them from having to move their feet."

When to Use

Anytime the teacher thinks it will help the student gain more bow control, except during the first few weeks of lessons. The conventional hold should be well established before this mini-game is played.

Inner Game

The teacher knows that a master string player can always control the tip of his bow. This essential technique is emphasized and improved through this mini-game because no one would want the imaginary sparrows to become frightened!

Team Tactics

Every string student can give the sparrows a ride.

The Groovy String
Mini-Game 43

Outer Game

The teacher points to a place on the string which she believes would be a better basic contact point for the bow hair than the one the student is currently using. It will probably be closer to the bridge, because most beginning cello students have a tendency to allow their bows to drift toward the fingerboard.

"Think of the string as having a deep groove cut into it. Let your bow sink into this groove. Now let's hear you play on this groovy string!"

When to Use

1. To make the student more conscious of the sounding point.
2. To move the contact point of his basic bow stroke closer to or farther from the bridge.
3. To keep the bow from drifting around on the string.
4. To help the student gain the kinesthetic sense of his bow sinking into the string.

Inner Game
The teacher recognizes that the location of a good bow contact point, often called the sounding point, is a major factor in deter-

mining the tone quality. Although this location, of course, will need to be varied in order to widen the range of colors in the student's tone palette, the first step in gaining bow control is to be able to keep the hair in one imaginary groove.

Since the string is more flexible and feels more cushiony near the fingerboard, most beginning cello students, especially the more sensitive ones, unconsciously prefer to draw the bow there. They further discover that the tone is more mellow and less likely to have a scratchy quality when they use this higher contact point. The teacher wishes to fight this natural but harmful tendency because it establishes the habit of suspending the weight of the right arm, since much less pressure is required when bowing near the fingerboard.

In the long-range game plan the student will have a much greater advantage if she learns from the beginning to *allow* the live weight of her arm to flow through her fingers to the bow stick so the hair will sink into the string. Later she can develop the skill of suspending some of the weight in order to produce a lighter, softer tone.

Reversing the procedure can be quite harmful. If the habit of suspending the arm weight is established during the early months of training, the student will find it extremely difficult to relax her arm. Instead, she will try to play louder by pushing down on the bow stick. This causes a harsh, ugly tone.

The analogy of the groovy string helps most students discover and identify with this important concept.

Team Tactics

The imaginary groove inspired by this outer game can also help the noncellists of the string class.

Honey on the Bow Stick
Mini-Game 44

Outer Game

Teacher: "Look! Someone smeared honey all over your bow stick and grip. Oh well, let's go ahead with your piece after all. Of course, your fingers will feel sticky, but that will make your tone more

beautiful. Sink into the string as you play."

When to Use

1. When the student's tone is harsh because she is grabbing at the bow with stiff, tense fingers.
2. When the student's tone is weak because her fingers are slipping around on the bow stick and grip.
3. When the student's tone is weak because she avoids playing loudly; she knows her tone is harsh when she plays forte and dislikes that quality.

Inner Game

The teacher recognizes that any word such as "honey," "rubber cement," or "molasses" will make the student's hand feel sticky and will automatically help her discover the clinging feeling so vital in producing beautiful tones. These are the key words in guiding the student to a combination of strength and flexibility. Mixed with other ingredients, such as the proper proportion of bow speed and distance from the bridge, the tone will become big and full but not harsh.

Team Tactics

Violinists, violists, and bassists will also benefit from the imaginary honey.

A Drop of Oil
Mini-Game 45

Outer Game

Teacher: "I'm going to place a drop of oil on the back of your right hand. When you bow near the tip, the oil should roll off on the thumb side of your hand."

When to Use

When the teacher observes that the student is not pronating her bow hand and forearm when playing near the tip.

Inner Game

This mini-game is another means of encouraging the student to tilt her hand and bow as she approaches the tip so that the weight of the bow will be focused back into the string. It is also important that the line between the elbow and the base knuckle of the second finger be straight; that is, the wrist should not be caved in, arched out, or twisted.

Should the imaginary drop of oil lose its magic with time, the teacher can advise the student to turn an invisible doorknob to the far left. This will place her forearm and hand in a pronated position suitable for playing at the tip.

Team Tactics

A Drop of Oil is useful in teaching pronation to all string students.

YOU Are There!
Mini-Game 46

Outer Game

Teacher: "Monkey see, monkey do!"

The teacher demonstrates how the bow can be placed on the string with the left hand directly above the sounding point, where the bow hair contacts the string.

"Push the stick down as close as possible to the hair. It will even touch the hair above the string unless it is near the frog or the tip. Make sure the bow is balanced perfectly between the two neighboring strings. While your left hand continues to hold the bow in this manner, place your right hand on the bow in the conventional bow hold. Position it in such a way that you will be able to keep the stick touching the hair at the sounding point even when you remove your left hand."

As the teacher touches the stick above the string, she adds: "Feel that *you* are there! Remove your left hand. Now, release some of the pressure on the stick as you start to pull your bow. . . .

"Remember exactly how your hand and arm feel so you can return to this position and feeling the next time you play in this part of your bow on this string. Focus your attention on the sounding point and feel that *you* are there!"

When to Use

1. Whenever the teacher believes that the student's arm and hand alignments would benefit from this emphasis on bow balance. It should precede Mini-Game

Mini-Game 47, *The Railroad Lantern*

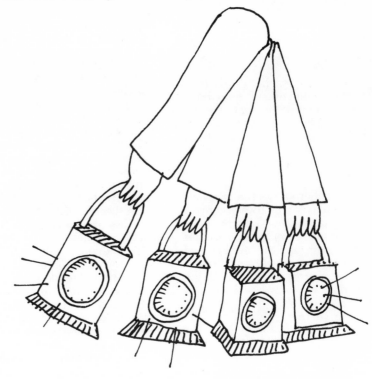

61, *Moon Landings*, and Mini-Game 66, *Can You Make a T Sound?*
2. Anytime as a preparation for martelé and staccato bowing.

Inner Game

This mini-game has the unique feature of reversing the usual procedure. Instead of holding the bow, then placing it on the string, the student positions the bow on the string with his left hand so that it balances perfectly; then his right hand and arm accommodate to its angle. Thus, the mini-game clearly demonstrates the optimum alignment of the hand, arm, and bow for the individual student when playing on each string in any part of the bow.

Team Tactics

You Are There! is designed for cello students.

The Railroad Lantern
Mini-Game 47

Outer Game

Teacher: "Have you ever been in a railroad yard at night to watch a train of boxcars being made up? If you haven't, it is done like this. The brakeman stands alongside

the rear of the train and signals to the engineer with a lantern. If he wants the engineer to move the train forward, he leisurely swings the lantern at arm's length forward and backward at his side. Try doing this while standing. Keep your elbow straight. . . . When he wants the engineer to stop, the brakeman swings the lantern back and forth in front of his body. Let's try doing this, keeping your elbow straight and the palm of your hand facing your body. Observe the way your upper arm swings.

"Now pantomime bowing long strokes in the air, keeping the same motion in your upper arm. Of course, now your elbow will not be kept straight. . . . Let's return to our instruments and hear you do this on your D string."

When to Use

Anytime the student's upper arm is not moving freely or his shoulder or elbow appears to be locked.

Inner Game

The goal is to have the student's upper arm move freely throughout the entire stroke. Frequently a student will immobilize his upper arm or lock his shoulder or elbow. The image of the lantern swinging in the darkness of the night helps the arm move naturally and freely.

Team Tactics

The Railroad Lantern is for cello and string bass students only.

Knock, Knock! Who's There?
Mini-Game 48

Outer Game

Teacher: "Place your bow so its hair at the tip is resting on the D string. Hold it there firmly with your *left* hand.

"Now, make a fist with your right hand. Knock gently on the top of the stick as though you are knocking on a door. Try doing this on all parts of the stick—at the tip, in the middle, and near the frog. As your hand and arm move farther away from your body, you will tilt your forearm and hand so only the first and second fingers contact the wood.

"Good! Now let's hear you bow on the D string, keeping the same relationship between your hand and arm as when you were knocking."

After this is done successfully, the mini-game will be repeated on each string.

When to Use

Anytime the teacher believes it will help the student perceive the proper alignment of the bow arm and hand.

Inner Game

This mini-game appeals to certain students and will aid them in their home practice. The teacher recognizes the importance of having a good alignment of the bow arm and hand; he also knows that the familiar act of knocking insures that the power line is free from the student's back to her hand, although the impulse will be felt in the hand. Certainly no one knocks on a door with a hand action completely isolated from the arm. In most cases, if a student discovers that her knock becomes weak and ineffective as her hand moves away from her body, she will quickly adjust her elbow so that the knocking action becomes more forceful.

Team Tactics

This mini-game is for cello and bass students only.

The Cushioned Elbow
Mini-Game 49

Outer Game

Teacher: "When you play at the frog, your arm is situated in such a comfortable position that it feels like there is a pillow under your elbow. In fact, the point of your elbow sinks into the feathers!"

When to Use

1. During the first weeks of lessons.
2. Whenever the teacher observes that the student's upper right arm is high or that his elbow is pointing out when he plays near the frog.

Inner Game

The teacher knows that, if the student picked up an object directly in front of him at the level of his bow, this action would place his elbow in a natural position. It is only when the student moves his hand and arm in an up-bow motion that he often fails to return his elbow to this position. Bowing with an elbow that always points out—resembling ironing—should be avoided because of its adverse ef-

Mini-Game 49, *The Cushioned Elbow*

fect on the tone. The very act of thinking of the underside of his elbow sinking into a feather pillow will relax the student's bow arm. He may need to be reminded to support his wrist.

Team Tactics

Though a cellist positions his bow arm differently from those playing the violin or viola, an imaginary pillow is a useful prop for the student who has a tendency to hold her arm excessively high.

The Follow-Through
Mini-Game 50

Outer Game

Teacher: "Let's be athletes today! We need some tennis players, golfers, and baseball batters!"

After a few imaginary balls are hit with style, the teacher calls attention to the follow-through of the stroke after the ball is contacted. The students will note that the racket (or club or bat) and the arm continue to move through the air in the same direction as the ball.

This action is then transferred to cello playing—through a series of down-bows, then up-bows, and finally to legato strokes in alternating directions. It will be noted, for example, that the hand continues to flow near the end of a down-bow, while the arm prepares for an up-bow stroke.

When to Use

At the teacher's discretion in order to improve the legato playing of his students or the ringing quality of a note followed by a rest.

Inner Game

The teacher knows the importance of the concept of the follow-through for effective legato playing, even though it is usually not very visible to the audience except on certain last notes of a composition or phrase. On the other hand, the athletes' use of it is quite apparent; thus, this analogy can help the student.

Team Tactics

This mini-game is for all string students.

The Five-Lane Bowling Alley
Mini-Game 51

Outer Game

Teacher: "Think of the space between the end of your fingerboard and your bridge as being crossed by a five-lane bowling alley.

"Try drawing your bow in lane one, which is nearest the fingerboard. To produce a beautiful tone, you will need to move it rather fast and lightly. Picture a lightweight bowling ball moving quickly and staying in its lane."

The teacher will guide the students in their exploration of each of the five lanes. It will be discovered that the bow must move heavier and slower in the lanes closer to the bridge.

"In order to produce beautiful sounds in lane five, your hand and arm will need to feel relaxed and heavy so your bow sinks down into the string; otherwise you will make squeaky sounds. Think of a large, heavy bowling ball moving slowly down the center of its lane, never getting near the gutters."

When to Use

1. To help the student bow parallel to the bridge.
2. To discover the varying weights and speeds required as the bow makes contact with the string at various distances from the bridge.
3. To discover the various tone qualities produced by bowing at different sounding points.
4. To correct the bad habit of always playing in one lane.
5. To correct the bad habit of shifting lanes indiscriminately.

Inner Game

The teacher recognizes that the very act of trying to stay in a specified lane will help the student gain bow control and keep her bow more parallel to the bridge. Also, her fingers, hand, and arm will soon learn to gauge the weight and speed in order to produce the desired sound.

Team Tactics
The Five-Lane Bowling Alley is applicable to all stringed instruments.

A Magic Trick: Feeling through an Object
Mini-Game 52

Outer Game

Teacher: "Have you ever stopped to think what a remarkable instrument your hand is? It not only moves in almost all directions, but it's good for pushing, pulling, grasping, and many other actions."

Together the students and the teacher discover all the many things a hand can do . . . pinch, stretch, soothe, pat, pound, caress, etc. The teacher leads the students into discovering that one of the greatest miracles is that the hand can *feel*. It has the ability to flash instant messages to the brain that something is rough, silky, velvety, sharp, hard, soft, spongy, and so on. Together they feel everything in sight—hair, fabrics, wood, steel, skin, plastic, etc.

"Now look at my billfold—the poor thing has no feeling at all. It just sits there. It can't feel whether it's in my purse, pocket, or hand, or whether it's sitting on velvet or sandpaper. But wait! Let me show you a bit of magic.

"I can hold my billfold in such a manner that I can feel an object right through it. As I stroke this desk with my billfold, it is almost as though the nerves of my fingers have grown right through the billfold and are feeling the wood. I can distinguish the difference between the desk and this rug."

The teacher hands her billfold and other objects to the students, and they feel everything in sight *through* the objects. Gradually the teacher leads them to feeling items through the bow and finally to feeling the string through the bow.

"Note that it's as though the bow is an extension of your hand and arm. Is the string soft or hard? Rigid or flexible? Try playing your cello while holding the bow in the same sensitive manner so you can feel the string as it vibrates. . . . Listen, isn't the sound beautiful when you play this way? It rings because the vibrations are free."

When to Use

Anytime except in the first lessons. It should be reserved until the student has a good start on bowing.

Mini-Game 55, The Dancing Bow

Inner Game

The teacher has experienced this sensation herself and knows that it is one of the keys to expressive string playing.

Team Tactics

All students of bowed instruments can play this mini-game.

The Standing Cellist
Mini-Game 53

Outer Game

The teacher asks the students to bow some rich full open strings while standing with their cellos.

"Let your bow sink into the string. . . . Good! Now sit down and try to match this same big vibrant sound."

Usually the sitting student will discover that his tone is decidedly smaller than the one he produced when standing.

"Try playing again while standing up. Then see if you can retain the same feeling in your arm and back when sitting."

When to Use

Whenever the teacher feels that the student and his cello are capable of producing a more vibrant, ringing sound.

Inner Game

The teacher knows from experience that almost all cello students can produce better tones on open strings when standing up. These tones can serve as models to emulate in home practice and are usually very effective in bringing about a noticeable improvement.

Team Tactics

This mini-game is for cello students only.

Bowing on the Finger
Mini-Game 54

Outer Game

The teacher demonstrates how the student can practice bowing silently by turning her bow upside-down and having the stick ride on her left index finger, which serves as a substitute string.

"Of course, with the bow upside-down you can't hold it exactly as you normally do, but it will help you practice bow distribution. For example, let's bow this rhythmic pattern of a quarter note followed by two eighths: whole bow, tip, tip."

When to Use

1. When introducing rhythmic patterns.
2. Anytime the teacher wishes some students in a class to practice silently so he can focus on listening to one student perform.

Inner Game

The teacher has learned that the student is better able to concentrate if she pantomimes a motion before actually performing it. This is especially true for rhythmic patterns involving the distribution of the bow in various ways. The sound itself seems to reduce the power of concentration at times.

This mini-game also serves as an effective means of occupying members of a class in a productive assignment while allowing the teacher to hear a solo performance. A piece of Kleenex under the right hand will protect the bow hair.

Team Tactics

All string students can play *Bowing on the Finger.*

The Dancing Bow
Mini-Game 55

Outer Game

Teacher: "Today we will really get acquainted with our bows. They are going to dance to music! Stand over here away from your cellos and hold your bows in the conventional manner."

To the background of music, the students move their bows in graceful arcs and semicircles, pretending that their bows are landing on clouds or foam rubber pillows at the end of each motion.

"Let your bow glide, soar, and dive in any manner you wish. Imagine it is an extension of your arm and hand!"

When to Use

1. After several months of study.
2. Anytime the student appears uncomfortable with his bow.

Inner Game

This mini-game can help the student learn to maneuver his bow with greater ease and to make it feel less like a foreign object. If the teacher makes sure that the bows are held in a good manner and that the motions are curved and flowing, the experience will be creative and productive.

The dancing bow can resemble the bouncing ball above the words of the old sing-along movies.

Team Tactics

All members of the string class can make their bows dance.

Pulling an Up-Bow
Mini-Game 56

Outer Game

Teacher: "Today we will learn the cellist's secret for achieving the same beautiful tone with long up-bows as with long down-bows. Since most of us produce our best tones while pulling the bow across the string in what is called the down-bow, it helps if we can acquire this same feeling of pulling when moving it in the up-bow direction. I know it sounds strange to pull something that is ahead of you, but today I'll show you how.

"Hold the bow at the frog in the conventional manner. Pull a long down-bow a few inches above the string. Freeze! While keeping your right hand still, use your left hand to reverse the direction of the bow so the wood near the frog is still in your right hand but the tip extends to the right. Now pull an up-bow in the air.

"This is exactly the feeling we should try to achieve when we draw an up-bow. As your arm pulls your hand, your hand will pull the bow!

"Let's play a series of down- and up-bows, making them all sound alike. Imagine that someone blindfolded is listening to you. Don't let him guess which direction you are bowing!"

When to Use

Whenever a student's up-bows do not have the same quality of sound as her down-bows.

Inner Game

The purpose of this mini-game is to help the student discover how to make an up-bow have the same tonal characteristics as a down-bow. Though some cello students respond well to the familiar words "pull" and "push" in describing the down- and up-bow actions, others will produce tones that are markedly different. This mini-game is especially beneficial to these students.

It must be noted that resistance is a necessary ingredient of the pulling action; thus, it is important for the bow to sink into the string before it is pulled. The fingers and hand will feel passive during these long sustained strokes, although there will be times when a string player's hand will feel active when producing fast or articulated strokes. The ear and the imagination of the player must serve as the final determiners of the physical actions to be used.

Team Tactics

Though many string teachers prefer the words "pull" and "push" when referring to down- and up-bows, the principle of striving to make them sound alike applies to all stringed instruments. This mini-game as described, however, is for cello and bass students.

Swatting Flies
Mini-Game 57

Outer Game

The teacher distributes a real or imaginary fly swatter to each student.

"Someone must have left the windows open—this place is swarming with flies! Swat them!"

While the flies are being swatted, the teacher notes:

"Look how you swat! Your hand and swatter flip back after you've hit the fly! They make a quick round trip from one spurt of energy!

"We use this rebound action when we play a very short note followed by a longer note on a separate bow. For example, when we play a sixteenth note with a down-bow, followed by a dotted eighth note on an up-bow, the second note results from the thrust of the down-bow. We are hearing the return trip!

"Our music will have much more rhythmic vitality if we remember to swat flies. If we forget to use rebound action and instead think of two separate motions producing these two notes, they will have a 'chug-chug' sound.

"Let's practice swatting flies to music! Be sure to make it clear whether you are swatting flies on up-bows or down-bows."

The teacher will perform suitable music on the piano or his instrument while the students swat flies in rhythm.

When to Use

To teach the rebound action required by various rhythmic patterns involving changes in bow direction. These include a sixteenth note or thirty-second note followed by a note of longer value.

Inner Game

The teacher recognizes that most students will not utilize the rebound action unless their attention is called to it. Through the simple act of swatting flies and relating it to string playing, the rhythmic vitality of a composition can be richly enhanced. This mini-game is especially useful in teaching hooked bowing.

Team Tactics

Swatting Flies is good for every string student.

The Mental Speedometer
Mini-Game 58

Outer Game

Teacher: "Every fine string player has a mental speedometer that helps him gauge the necessary speed of his bow strokes. As you progress and play more advanced music, you will have many gradations of bow speed.

"For now let's examine the rhythmic pattern of a half note followed by a quarter in this waltz. Try playing the half note at thirty miles per hour and the quarter note at sixty, but adjust your arm weight so the quarter note sounds just as beautiful as the half note."

When to Use

Whenever the teacher wishes to call attention to the desirability or the necessity of a change in bow speed.

Inner Game

The teacher recognizes that this analogy is meaningful to almost all students. Thus, a reference to the relative miles per hour of various bow strokes is an aid to communication.

Team Tactics

This mini-game is for all string students.

Skywriting
Mini-Game 59

Outer Game

The teacher asks the student to write her name in the air with the tip of her bow while holding it in the conventional manner.

The goal is to exert such fine control over the movement of the bow tip that it is as though the bow is an extension of the player's arm and the tip is an imaginary index finger writing in the sky.

When to Use

Anytime after several months of study in order to help the student gain better bow control.

Inner Game

The teacher recognizes that any game or exercise which emphasizes the student's control over the tip of her bow will improve her playing.

Team Tactics

Skywriting is for all members of the string class.

The Recipe for a Big Tone
Mini-Game 60

Outer Game

Teacher: "The recipe for a big tone when you're playing open strings contains three ingredients:

1. The distribution of pressure (of the right kind!) on the bow stick.
2. A good contact point on the string.
3. The speed of the bow as it is pulled parallel to the bridge.

The quantity of each ingredient is determined by experimentation and guided by the musician's ear. Altering the amount of one ingredient will change one or both of the others proportionately.

"Blend all ingredients well. Temper with the sensitive ear."

When to Use

Anytime except in the very beginning lessons.

Inner Game

This mini-game is just another way of expressing the basic princi-

ples of tone production. The teacher may wish to substitute the word "weight" for "pressure" if she believes it will have a more positive effect on the student. At some point she will call attention to the fact that the thickness and length of the string also affect the recipe.

The reader may wish to refer to Mini-Game 51, *The Five-Lane Bowling Alley*, at this time.

Team Tactics

The exact recipe will vary for each stringed instrument, but the ingredients will be the same.

Moon Landings
Mini-Game 61

Outer Game

The students find a perfect bow balance and an optimum position of the right arm and hand by playing Mini-Game 46, *YOU Are There!*

Teacher: "Lift your bow high off the string, keeping it at the same angle. Let's practice setting it back down on the identical sounding point as gently as Neil Armstrong had to land his lunar module on the surface of the moon. . . .

"Let's practice moon landings in various other parts of your bow. Imagine a little lunar module sitting on a selected spot on your stick, then lower it directly to the string from above. Let it sink gently into the moon dust."

When to Use

1. Early in the training after Mini-Game 46, *YOU Are There!*
2. Whenever the teacher believes it will help the student find a better angle of the bow for playing in its various parts or improve his hand and arm alignment.

Inner Game

The teacher's goal is to help the student find the perfect balance of his bow when playing in various parts of it and on different strings. When performed successfully, the bow and the player's arm should be in a good position to produce sounds starting with t. See Mini-Game 66, *Can You Make a T Sound?*

Team Tactics

All members of the string class can play *Moon Landings*.

Pulling through a Milkshake
Mini-Game 62

Outer Game

The students sit with their cellos in a good playing position. The teacher checks to be sure that their shoulders are not twisted and their body weight is leaned slightly forward.

"Imagine that the room is filled with a creamy chocolate milkshake

Mini-Game 62, Pulling through a Milkshake

that comes almost up to your chest! Pull your hand through the milkshake as though you are pulling a down-bow. Doesn't it remind you of swimming? Now pull some up-bows!

"Always remember that the most beautiful singing cello tones are produced by pulling the bow. If you pull your hand, the bow will be pulled. Let's hear you play now."

When to Use

Anytime the teacher wishes to emphasize the importance of using a pulling action in bowing.

Inner Game

The teacher knows that almost every youngster has experienced swimming. The milkshake was substituted for water in order to provide more resistance, a vital ingredient of the desired pulling action.

By modifying this mini-game to demonstrate both good and bad postures, the teacher can emphasize the importance of not twisting the shoulders. After the students have pantomimed bowing through the imaginary milkshake, the teacher can ask them to repeat it with their right shoulders swung forward. Almost invariably the students will laugh because the pulling action completely eludes them in this incorrect posture.

The reader may wish to refer to the inner game explanation of Mini-Game 56, *Pulling an Up-Bow*, at this time.

Team Tactics

Though the pulling action is important in violin and viola playing, this mini-game as described is for cello and bass students.

What's My String?
Mini-Game 63

Outer Game

Teacher: "Everyone except Cathy, close your eyes! Cathy, place your bow near the frog on any string of your choice. . . . OK, everyone, open your eyes!"

The students will discover that the teacher is holding a paper or some music over Cathy's right hand and the space between her fingerboard and bridge.

"Ted and Mark, can you guess which string she has chosen? Look at the height of her right elbow and the angle of her bow."

When to Use

Whenever the teacher wants to call attention to the arm level required by each string.

Inner Game

This mini-game makes the students more acutely aware of the different levels of the right arm. It also gives the performing student the responsibility of being in a good playing position so the cues will be reliable.

Team Tactics

What's My String? is for all string students.

Resist Me!
Mini-Game 64

Outer Game

After the student places his bow on the string, the teacher makes an attempt to pull it away from the string by gently tugging on the bow stick either directly above the sounding point or at the bow tip.

"Resist me! Keep the bow on the string!"

When to Use

When the bow has a tendency to slip around on the string.

Inner Game

This action on the part of the teacher causes the student to focus his attention on the spot where the bow contacts the string. Unconsciously the student will adjust the angle of the bow, his bow hold, and/or his hand and arm alignment so the hair sinks deeper into the string, resulting in better tone production. In general, the line formed by the back of the hand should conform to the same slant as the bow stick.

Team Tactics

Resist Me! can be played by all members of the string class but is particularly helpful to cello and bass students because their thicker strings have a tendency to produce

a surface sound if bow contact is not good.

The Trolley Car Ride
Mini-Game 65

Outer Game

The class pretends it is taking a trolley car ride up and down the hills of San Francisco. The students are standing behind the teacher, who plays the role of the driver. When the teacher slams on the brakes, all her passengers lean forward in the direction the trolley car has been moving.

Teacher: "This is the way we feel when we bow legato strokes. As we near the end of an up-bow, even though we know we are going to start a down-bow, there is something that makes us want to move just a little bit farther in the up-bow direction. The same is true as we finish a down-bow.

"Let's try this with our instruments."

When to Use

Anytime, except in the very early training, the teacher believes it will help the student gain the concept of what Carl Flesch termed "stroke-continuation."

Inner Game

In *The Art of Violin Playing*, Carl Flesch pointed out the peculiar process that takes place in the bow change. He wrote that "it seems as though there exists some physical necessity which prevents us from changing the bow stroke before we have added a small portion to the one coming to the end." He continued by citing an example involving a moving trolley car.

Team Tactics

The Trolley Car Ride is for all members of the string class.

Can You Make a T Sound?
Mini-Game 66

Outer Game

Teacher: "In music, as in speech, it is important to have both vowels and consonants. T is a particularly vital sound because it helps us in accents and articulations. In fact,

Mini-Game 66, *Can You Make a T Sound?*

siveness. The teacher's goal is to help the student produce music which seems as though it has words. At times she may even suggest imitation of the sounds of certain words, such as "rose," "mum," or "broken."

Team Tactics

This mini-game is applicable to all stringed instruments.

The Rubber Bow Bumpers
Mini-Game 67

Outer Game

Teacher: "Imagine that your bow has a three-inch-thick soft rubber bumper on each end and that you are seated very near to a wall on your right. Place the bow on the string near the tip and give it a quick down stroke. Watch it rebound off the wall!

"Now move the imaginary wall to your left and place your bow on the string near the frog. Give it a quick up stroke. Watch it rebound!

"The rebound action is often used in string playing, especially when a short note is followed by a long note on a separate bow. The fast short stroke will be initiated by you, but the longer note following it will be taken care of by the rebound action off the wall. Let's practice this on open strings, then try it on your piece."

When to Use

When the teacher wishes to stress the bow's rebound action, particularly in dotted rhythms.

Inner Game

The rebound action plays a vital role in bowing, especially as the literature becomes more advanced. By introducing this action in the early training, the teacher insures that the bow hold, the approach, and the arm alignment are workable for such techniques as hooked bowing.

Team Tactics

Though the imaginary walls in this outer game are primarily useful to cello and bass students, the principles expressed apply to all stringed instruments.

a fine cellist is able to produce a sound starting with t in any part of his bow. Let's try this now.

"Place the middle of your bow on the string. Pinch the bow stick momentarily with your index finger and thumb so the wood touches the hair directly above the sounding point. Release the pinching action as you start the stroke.

"Practice making t sounds in all parts of the bow with both up and down strokes. Of course, the wood cannot touch the hair at the extreme ends of the bow. You can also practice making a series of t sounds going in one direction of the bow with short stops between them.

"Listen carefully!"

When to Use

1. Anytime after the student has a good start in bowing. This mini-game should be preceded by Mini-Game 46, *YOU Are There!*
2. Whenever articulated bowing is being emphasized.

Inner Game

The teacher recognizes not only that articulations are very important in music making but also that the act of producing a t sound is a good means of checking the angle of the bow and the hand and arm alignment. If the student produces a th sound instead of a t sound in any part of the bow, he realizes that something is wrong and should be corrected. This mini-game prepares the student for martelé and staccato bowing as well as accents.

Later the teacher can emphasize the production of other consonantal sounds such as d, p, m, and br as a means of developing expres-

The Secret Way to Cross Strings
Mini-Game 68

Outer Game

Teacher: "Today I'm going to help you discover a secret every master cellist knows. But first: Monkey see, monkey do!"

With the students mimicking her, the teacher rubs her forehead with her right hand, then scratches her head, pitches an imaginary baseball like a pro, swings a golf club, stamps her left foot on the floor, etc.

Soon she calls attention to the fact that every action of the body requires a preparatory action. After the brain sends a signal through the nerves telling the muscles and tendons what to do, the first step is a preparatory one. She points out that the golfer doesn't just hit the ball, he first swings the club backward before striking the ball with a forward motion. The head didn't get scratched until the hand arrived. The first step in stamping the foot was to lift it. She tells the students that these are called "preparatory" motions or actions.

Gradually the teacher leads the students back to cello playing. She shows them how a master cellist crosses strings with a curving motion. The arm, hand, and bow all work together as one unit. She points out that the preparatory action in the form of a curve takes place during the time value of the old note. In fact, the motion used for producing the old note now takes on a new contour as it flows into the preparatory action for the new note.

The teacher explains how a master cellist playing two notes on different strings quickly sizes up the distance between the perfect locations of the hand and arm for each of the two notes. He then gauges the time required for the preparatory curving action, and his elbow and arm will seem to float into the new level.

"Now let's play some examples of string crossings and see if large or small motions are required. Naturally you will have to begin the large ones sooner in order to arrive gracefully at the new destination on time."

When to Use

When the teacher feels that the student is ready for such a detailed study of string crossings. This will not be very early in the training, since the beginning student's first experience with string crossings will involve rests between the notes. Mini-Game 35, *Comparing the Air Corridors*, should precede this mini-game.

Inner Game

The teacher knows from experience that the preparatory action used in a specific technique plays a vital part in determining its success. In analyzing a problem, she is also aware that the first place to check is the preparatory motion.

In the case of crossing strings at the bow tip, for example, the new tone is apt to sputter if the direction of the new stroke is started before the new arm level is attained. The teacher recognizes the importance of timing: the preparatory action must be welded into the motion of the old note while it is still sounding.

Since preparatory motions used by cellists are for the most part not obvious, the teacher knows that the action images of a golfer or a baseball pitcher will evoke a clearer mental picture, thus helping the student identify with the concept.

Team Tactics

The principles regarding preparatory actions are the same for all stringed instruments.

The Gold Brick
Mini-Game 69

Outer Game

Teacher: "When you play at the frog, let your upper arm be near your body and your elbow point down. If you see your elbow sticking out, attach an imaginary gold brick to it so that it sinks into place.

"Of course, the elbow will be at a different level for each string, but it should always feel relaxed when you play at the frog. Let your upper arm hang loose."

When to Use

When the teacher notices that the student's right elbow is hiked up in an awkward position.

Inner Game

The teacher recognizes that it is important for the wrist to be supported so the live weight can be channeled through the fingers to the bow stick. However, he knows that many beginning cello students tend to hike up their elbows in an awkward fashion; this causes tension and can destroy the beauty of the tone.

Team Tactics

Though this mini-game is especially for cellists, the teacher may find imaginary gold bricks and beanbags handy tools in the string class.

The Trampoline
Mini-Game 70

Outer Game

Teacher: "First focus your attention on one magic spot on your bow. Pretend your string is a trampoline. Now, using your entire arm in a springing motion, throw that spot to the string and let your arm and bow bounce right back up!

"The height of the bounce is not important—what's vital is that both the frog and the tip ends of the bow spring up the same distance."

The students will repeat this almost silent springing action in various parts of the bow by simply shifting the magic spot around on the stick. Each string will serve as a trampoline.

When to Use

In the early training as a means of achieving better bow balance and setting up pre-spiccato conditions.

Inner Game

This mini-game offers a primitive sample of the actions required in some more advanced techniques. By having her student perform it in the early weeks of study, the teacher is testing and insuring the workability of his position and approach.

Team Tactics

The Trampoline is for all members of the string class.

A Real Bouncer—the Spiccato
Mini-Game 71

Outer Game

Teacher: "Monkey see, monkey do!"

Holding a pencil in his hand like a baton, the teacher begins swinging it back and forth as though he is outlining the bottom of a dinner plate.

"Notice how balanced our arms and hands feel! Since one swing leads into the next, we could probably do this all day without getting tired. It is all done through rebounds."

"Let's move to this table and continue swinging, allowing the pencil to hit the tabletop at the bottom of each arc."

Soon the teacher and the students return to their cellos. While holding their bows at the balance point, they continue to outline the lower portion of a plate, hitting the D string at the bottom of each swing. Gradually the speed is quickened and the dinner plate shrinks to a saucer, then to a coffee cup.

"This spiccato bowing is a real bouncer!"

When the teacher thinks it appropriate, the student's hand will move to the conventional bow hold. The string will still be contacted by the hair at the balance point of the bow, however.

When to Use

When introducing spiccato bowing. This mini-game should be preceded by Mini-Game 70, *The Trampoline*.

Inner Game

The teacher's goal is to help the student gain the sensation of the swinging rebound action before applying it to the instrument, thereby improving the chances for success. The mini-game will be repeated on each string with the imaginary dishes hung at the appropriate angles. In each case the teacher will make sure that the bow is thrown from above so that a bouncing action will result.

Team Tactics

This procedure of teaching spiccato bowing can also be used with violin, viola, and bass students.

The Flowing Scarves
Mini-Game 72

Outer Game

When the students are studying a composition that requires long, flowing bow strokes, such as a simple waltz, the teacher distributes a chiffon scarf to each member of the class. These are the thin, inexpensive head scarves available in most supermarkets.

While the teacher plays the composition on the piano, or possibly on his own stringed instrument, the students will hum the melody and pull the scarves through the air, following the indicated bowing patterns. This is most effective when each student is standing and is holding a corner of the scarf between the thumb and the second finger.

Teacher: "Notice how the scarf flows through the air as you pantomime pulling down- and up-bows, which in the case of cellists are actually to the right or to the left. Our bow strokes run either horizontally or at an angle to the floor, depending on the string we are playing on; as you know, we use the same terms as our violinist friends.

"Begin each up-bow at a slightly higher level than the end of the preceding down-bow. Imagine your hand and scarf are moving up around a stick of peppermint suspended in the air at the same angle you would hold a bow. See how your scarf continues to flow in the down-bow direction as your arm prepares and even begins the up-bow? Try to get this same flowing motion when you play. It's almost like liquid flowing without any stop in the motion as you change direction."

When to Use

When the teacher believes it is time to emphasize flowing, legato bow strokes.

Inner Game

The teacher is aware that this mini-game helps make visible the characteristics associated with legato strokes. In her effort to keep the scarf flowing and continuously moving, the student will gain the feeling of the muscular action required in changing bow directions.

In addition, this mini-game helps the student discover or reinforce the sensation of a flowing motion in her hand and bow. When this feeling is transferred to cello playing, the tone will be greatly enhanced. The reader may wish to refer to Mini-Game 36, *The Big Full Moon*, and Mini-Game 56, *Pulling an Up-Bow*, at this time.

Team Tactics

This mini-game is for all string students.

Knee Writing
Mini-Game 73

Outer Game

The teacher guides the student into writing his name across his right knee with the end of the screw while he holds the bow in the conventional manner. His wrist will be implanted on his right leg so that the entire action is restricted to his supple fingers. The letters, of course, will be very small.

When to Use

Anytime the teacher wishes to stress finger flexibility in the bow hand; however, it should not be done in the early part of the training.

Inner Game

The teacher knows the importance of finger flexibility in the bow hold and that this type of activity will improve it. In fact, many students will not be able to accomplish this on their first attempt.

Since *Knee Writing* focuses the student's attention on the outer extremities of the body and the refinement of motion, it is generally better to postpone this mini-game until the big motions are well established.

Team Tactics

All members of the string class can benefit from *Knee Writing* but, of course, it is necessary for them to be seated.

Spread the Peanut Butter
Mini-Game 74

Outer Game

Teacher: "Stick out the little finger of your left hand so I can put a glob of imaginary peanut butter on its inner side near the tip. Now insert it between the bow hair and stick, and pantomime bowing so the peanut butter spreads smoothly all over the bottom part of the bow stick. Your inserted finger should feel the same pressure when you bow at the tip as at the frog.

"This is the way your string feels when you bow. It feels too, you know! If your tone is weak at the tip, remember to trace the bottom of the big full moon. Note the angle of your forearm and bow stick when you do this.

"Let's hear you play some open strings now, keeping this same feeling. This time imagine that I have put a dab of peanut butter on the string itself. Spread it all through the bow hair as you play. This will help you make a beautiful sound, and your tone will be as big when you play at the tip as at the frog."

When to Use

1. After the student has a good start on bowing. It should be preceded by Mini-Game 36, *The Big Full Moon*.
2. Whenever the teacher notes that the student's tone is weak

when she plays in the upper half of her bow or the student's tone is weak because her fingers are not sinking into the top of the stick.

3. Anytime the teacher wishes to occupy part of the class in a productive silent endeavor so he can concentrate on the playing of one student.

Inner Game

The teacher knows that, through this mini-game, the student will better understand the function of the bow. Since the little finger of her left hand plays the role of the string, the student can immediately detect when not enough pressure is focused into it. Thus, she is better able to correct specific weaknesses in the flow and distribution of weight.

Should the student not understand the concept of adjusting the angle of her bow and right hand and arm when playing at the tip, she will try to compensate for the lack of natural weight by pushing her fingers hard against the bow stick. This is ineffective, of course, and the tone will remain weak despite an excessive use of energy.

Team Tactics

In principle this mini-game is applicable to all stringed instruments but, because of the narrow distance between the hair and the stick in violin and viola bows, there is often not enough space for a finger. Rather than having violin and viola students warm the bench, the teacher may prefer that they spread the peanut butter on the opposite side of the stick while holding it in the upside-down position described in Mini-Game 54, *Bowing on the Finger*.

The Hummingbird
Mini-Game 75

Outer Game

The teacher draws, or pantomimes drawing, her bow across the D string, stops it, then lifts her right hand and bow several inches above the string and shakes them up and down in a wide fluttering motion.

"It's a hummingbird! He is hovering over a bright red geranium and is trying to decide whether or not to take a sip! Let's see you do this."

Should the student have difficulty in controlling his bow tip while waving his hand and bow frog in this fast vertical motion, he can quickly adjust his bow hold to make it easier. The tip will show some motion, of course, but it will be very gentle and always remain in its air corridor. Though the impulse will be in the student's hand, his entire arm should be allowed to move and feel very free.

"Now let's play your piece again. When I call out 'bird!' stop the tone and fly—no matter what part of the bow you are playing in."

When to Use

1. After the student has played several months and has a good start on bowing technique.
2. Whenever the teacher observes one of the following: the student's bow arm looks tense and awkward; the balance in his right hand does not appear centered in the second finger and thumb; or there is not a straight line between the elbow and the base knuckle of the second finger when the student plays near the tip.

Inner Game

The teacher recognizes that the act of waving or shaking the hand up and down rapidly while holding the bow is an excellent way to check the position of the hand and arm. If they are not properly aligned in relation to the bow or if tension is present in any part of the arm, a fluttering motion can be difficult to execute. Furthermore, proper control of the bow tip will be impossible.

She is also aware that some vertical action in the right hand is essential for expressive string playing and that this mini-game samples an important motion that is vital in advanced technique.

The Hummingbird should be played on each string. The shaking action will always be at a 90° angle to the bow stick. Though the player's attention will be focused on his right hand, his loose upper arm will also move.

As a variation of this outer game, the hand can flutter over the entire air corridor of each string in the direction of down- and up-bows. It is as though the little bird is flying back and forth above a row of pink petunias. The garden can be situated on a slope when the A or the C string is involved. The reader is advised to refer to Mini-Game 35, *Comparing the Air Corridors*, at this time.

Team Tactics

This mini-game can be adapted to any stringed instrument.

What the Bow Stick Feels
Mini-Game 76

Outer Game

Teacher: "Let's pretend that one of your index fingers is a bow stick. Hold your hand rather rigidly with the thumb side up and I'll show you what my bow would feel if it were alive."

The teacher shapes his own right hand in the position of a good bow hold and places it on the student's finger, which serves as a substitute bow stick. Then the teacher tugs his own hand in the up-bow direction. Though there will be some motion, his fingers will not leave the places where they initially contacted the student's index finger. The teacher then tugs in the direction of a down-bow. This gives the impression to both teacher and student that the teacher's fingers are stuck; yet they both can feel the direction of the attempted pull.

"Now let's change roles. You be the player and my index finger will be the bow stick. Show me what your bow stick feels."

When to Use

Anytime the teacher believes it would help the student discover the sensation of weight flowing through the clinging fingers of the bow hand and the difference between the up-bow and down-bow sensations.

Inner Game

This mini-game, which takes only a few seconds, can immediately communicate to the student a desirable approach to holding and pulling the bow. On the other hand, when the roles are reversed, the teacher is able to detect instantly if the student has gained the kinesthetic sense. When the player pulls an up-bow, her fingers will become straighter and will feel somewhat stretched; in the down-bow action they will curve gently around the bow stick. The actions will not initiate in the fingers; rather they are *allowed* to change shape.

Team Tactics

Every member of the string class can play this mini-game.

The Door Spring
Mini-Game 77

Outer Game

Teacher: "Let's attach an imaginary door spring—a coiled wire—to each end of your bow, Nancy. . . . Now I'll hold the one attached to the tip while you pull a down-bow. Can you feel the resistance?

"Now I'll stand on your right side and hold the coiled spring attached to the frog. Pull an up-bow while imagining the resistance it offers."

When to Use

Anytime, not too early in the training, the teacher wishes to stress the pulling action of the bow arm.

Inner Game

Though the teacher will never touch the bow, the feeling of suction between the bow hair and the string will be intensified because of the student's imagination.

Since a pulling action in the bow arm produces a beautiful singing string tone, and a good pull is dependent on resistance, this mental game usually brings about a marked improvement in the tone quality.

Team Tactics

All string students can play this mini-game. Although many teachers prefer the word "push" when referring to the up-bow action, the imaginary door spring still offers an effective resistance as the bow is moved away from it.

The F♯ String
Mini-Game 78

Outer Game

Teacher: "When we play fast passages which require crossing back and forth between two strings, it helps to imagine that the bow is balanced on an invisible third string halfway between the two strings. By doing so, your hand and arm do not have to move so far. Between A and D, for example, picture an F♯ string!"

When to Use

When playing passages which involve crossing back and forth rapidly between two strings.

Inner Game

The teacher's goal is to help the student minimize the motion required in changing arm levels by finding a midpoint balance. An imaginary third string will enable the student to play this type of passage much more rapidly and gracefully.

Team Tactics

An invisible string can help all string students.

Painting
Mini-Game 79

Outer Game

Teacher: "Often a master cellist feels like she is painting when she bows. Without your bow, try painting the air purple. Note how free and fluid your fingers feel. They resemble the bristles of a brush!

"Now hold the bow on the A string with your left hand, and paint the top of the bow stick. Your movements will be silky smooth."

The teacher will proceed to guide the student in transferring this feeling back to his cello playing.

When to Use

Whenever the teacher wishes to emphasize the fluidity of the bow strokes.

Inner Game

The teacher knows that this analogy is meaningful to most students and can greatly enhance the tone quality. She will take care that the painting action does not initiate in the fingers but, rather, is allowed to happen because of the arm motion and the flexibility of the fingers and wrist.

Team Tactics

Painting will help all members of the string class.

The Soft Rubber Bow
Mini-Game 80

Outer Game

Teacher: "Today I brought several kinds of fabric. I'd like you to feel and describe them to me."

The students feel and discuss pieces of scratchy burlap, soft velveteen, smooth silk, etc.

"Now let's hear your piece again. As you play, try to find that same sensitive spot in your fingers and imagine that the bow stick is made of soft rubber. This doesn't mean that you will play softer; in fact, you can play quite loudly.

"Remember this: the relationship between the bow hair and the string will reflect the same relationship that exists between your fingers and the bow stick. You are dealing with four flexible objects: the string, the bow hair, the bow stick, and your fingers. If your fingers sink into the bow stick, the hair will sink into the string; thus, your tone will be beautiful and free. If your fingers grab the bow stick and are rigid and stiff, your tone will be hard and stiff. Concentrate on sinking into that soft rubber bow while you play your piece again."

When to Use

1. Anytime the teacher detects a hard quality in the student's tone.
2. Whenever the student's fingers appear rigid and stiff.
3. Anytime the student's tone lacks sensitivity.

Inner Game

The teacher's goal is to help his student express the beauty within her through her cello and he recognizes that a beautiful and sensitive tone is the first criterion. He is aware that the creation of such a tone is impossible unless the player is *physically* sensitive to her cello and bow. He has further concluded that in no aspect of life does insensitivity breed sensitivity.

Team Tactics

This mini-game applies to all stringed instruments.

Roping the Bow Arm
Mini-Game 81

Outer Game

Teacher: "Place the tip of your bow firmly on the string. It should feel as though the hair has been Scotch-taped to it. . . . I'm tying an imaginary rope around your right forearm just above the wrist. Now let's see what happens when I pull on the rope."

The teacher pantomimes pulling the imaginary rope so that the student's arm and bow move in an up-bow motion.

"Listen to the beautiful sound! Watch how your arm changes its shape throughout the entire stroke! At any moment you could easily stop playing and wave good-bye while still holding your bow!"

When to Use

Anytime in the training, especially when the student's up-bows sound different from his down-bows.

Inner Game

The primary purpose of this mini-game is to help the student gain the feeling of up-bow action. The teacher recognizes that her pantomimed gesture is dramatic enough that it will easily be remembered. The added checkpoint of waving good-bye while holding the bow is a means of insuring that the arm and hand are properly aligned and that the balance of the hand remains in the second finger and thumb.

Team Tactics

All string students can play *Roping the Bow Arm*.

APPROACHES TO ESTABLISHING THE BOW HOLD BY COMBINING MINI-GAMES

Four approaches to establishing a good cello bow hold by using various combinations of mini-games are presented in this section. *The Strawberry-Picking Approach*, for example, is a composite of ten mini-games previously presented. Information regarding each approach's adaptability to the other stringed instruments is given under the heading "Team Tactics."

Since effective teaching in the early lessons requires constant review, particularly with regard to positions of the body in relation to the instrument and the bow, these approaches are intended to serve as alternatives to those given in the student's method book. It is generally recognized that when a problem arises in the bow hold it is advantageous to remove the bow from the student's hand and start again from the beginning.

The Palm Reader Approach

Outer Game

The student sits with her cello in a good position.

Teacher: "Hold out your right hand so I can read your palm. Ah, I see a happy future! You and your bow will become good friends because it will help you express yourself through music! Try easing your fingers a little farther apart so there is an air space between each one."

The teacher lays the bow across the student's fingers so that her second finger is near the bow's balance point. From the student's vantage, the frog will be to the left of her hand, the hair will face upward, and the stick will cross the first and second fingers between their first two joints. It will contact the third finger at its first joint and the fourth finger about halfway between the tip and the first joint.

"Now curve all your fingers gently and place the tip of your thumb on the side of the stick opposite your second finger. The thumb will probably be gently curved outward or, at least, not caved in. Adjust your fingers so they cling to the stick without touching the hair and the side of your first finger tilts toward the wood."

The teacher removes his own hand from the bow. "Turn your hand over so you can look at the back of it. Let me check it. . . . Good! Now we'll learn how to make the strings vibrate so your cello sings!"

Before the lesson ends, the teacher will show the student how to use her own left hand in laying the bow across her right fingers so she is not dependent on him.

When to Use

1. At the first lesson after the student has learned how to sit and to hold her cello.
2. Whenever the teacher believes a review is in order.

Inner Game

The teacher understands how eagerly the student wants to play her cello at the first lesson. This is usually the simplest approach to holding the bow and will aid in getting started immediately. If the teacher prefers, a pencil may be substituted for a bow in the initial approach since it is lighter and more familiar.

He also recognizes the advantages of the beginning student holding the bow at its balance point, where it feels the lightest and most manageable. The transfer to the conventional bow hold can easily be made later by using the left hand to slide the bow through the right hand until the tip of the thumb stops half on the hump of the frog and half on the wood. Though some adjustments in weight distribution will be made, the center balance of the hand will remain in the thumb and second finger.

The reader may wish to refer to the following mini-games used in this approach:
26, *Finding the Balance Point*
28, *The Bow Arm's Trusty Aide*

Team Tactics

This approach can be adapted to the violin and the viola, although the exact bow hold will be different from that of the cello. In teaching bass students it is generally considered preferable to begin with the conventional bow hold rather than at the balance point.

The Strawberry-Picking Approach

Outer Game

Teacher: "I'd like you to dip your right hand into this imaginary bucket of water. Since we have no towels, I guess you'll have to dry it by shaking off the water. . . .

"Freeze! Look how your hand is hanging. Notice the distance between your fingers. Remember how it looks and feels because this is exactly the right spacing for *your* fingers when *you* hold your cello bow. See how your little finger seems to grow right out of your hand as I trace the magic dotted line. . . . Take a photo. Click!

"OK, dip your hand into the water again. Shake it dry. . . . Freeze! Now let it dangle quietly while you pick that strawberry that is hanging below your second finger. . . . Hold it gently between the tip of your thumb and the pad or the first joint of your second finger. . . . Allow me to remove the strawberry and insert this pencil in its place. I'll initiate the action; you remain passive."

The teacher inserts the pencil horizontally, then pushes it up slightly so the student's passive, rounded fingers make contact with it. Each finger will touch the pencil. The first finger will lean on the wood between its first and second joints; the thumb will be curved gently outward or, at least, not caved in; the fourth finger pad will go slightly over the wood; and the third finger will fall naturally between the second and the fourth.

"Let's imagine that this yellow pencil is part of you. It's as though you were born with it. Think of it as a piece of your hand and arm. Now, without touching any surface, go through the motions you would use to polish furniture and clean windows. The contact points between your fingers and the pencil will remain the same. Notice how light the pencil feels. At the same time it is secure because it was dropped into a honey jar just before your lesson! Don't your fingers feel sticky and flexible?"

After all the imaginary walls, windows, and furniture are clean, the teacher will lead the student through the entire sequence again, except this time the cello bow will be substituted for the pencil. The teacher will insert it so the student's thumb and second finger are at the balance point of the bow.

Finally, the game is repeated with the student himself inserting the bow with the aid of his left hand.

When to Use

1. At one of the early lessons but not in the initial introduction of the bow hold.
2. Anytime the teacher believes a detailed review or an alternative approach would be beneficial.

Inner Game

The teacher's goal is to lead the student step by step to a bow hold that not only looks good but feels natural to the student. By isolating each step and relating it to an everyday experience, the teacher realizes that the chances for the student succeeding and feeling successful are heightened. Thus, the habit of success is being established and the seed of confidence planted.

This approach also has positive effects because it helps the student gain the feeling that the bow is an extension of his arm and hand, discover the natural spacing between his fingers, and find the balance of his hand by picking the strawberry. An added benefit is that he will not clamp his thumb and second finger because he does not want to bruise the strawberry. Later, when the teacher thinks it appropriate, the right hand will be moved to the conventional bow hold as described in the inner game of *The Palm Reader Approach*. If *The Strawberry-Picking Approach* is used as a review, the teacher may prefer to use the conventional hold in the initial introduction of this approach.

Since *The Strawberry-Picking Approach* is actually a sequence of ten mini-games, the reader may wish to refer to the inner game explanations of the following mini-games:

24, *The Dripping Wet Hand*
2, *Freeze!*
3, *The Magic Dotted Line*
4, *Take a Photo, Click!*
27, *Pick a Ripe Red Strawberry*
38, *The Magic Tool for Picking up Objects*
33, *Polishing the Furniture and Cleaning the Windows*
44, *Honey on the Bow Stick*
26, *Finding the Balance Point*
28, *The Bow Arm's Trusty Aide*

Team Tactics

The Strawberry-Picking Approach can easily be modified for teaching violin, viola, or string bass, although the exact placement of the fingers will be different from that of the cello bow hold.

The Ready Hand Approach

Outer Game

The student sits with her cello in a good position.

Teacher: "Dangle your right hand in the air like the clapper of a bell. Let it ring! Notice the spacing between your fingers. Keep that spacing but raise your hand slightly so it is easier to see your ring if you are wearing one.

"Now tap the first joint of your second finger gently against the tip of your thumb. Of course, all your fingers will move with it. Stop tapping and leave just enough space between your second finger and your thumb for a large purple grape."

The teacher brings up a bow between the student's thumb tip and fingers but does not allow it to touch them. He will keep it suspended so the bow's balance point is near the student's thumb.

"Can't you almost *feel* the bow? Your hand is ready for it. Now, take hold of it nicely. Note how your whole hand works as one unit and your first finger leans slightly on the stick between its first and second joints."

After the teacher checks the bow hold, the student will play some open strings, preferably one of the inner ones. Before the lesson is over, the teacher will show the student how she can use her left hand to hold the bow on the string while she prepares her right hand. Thus, she will not be dependent on the teacher.

When to Use

1. In an early lesson after the student has learned how to sit and to hold her cello.
2. Whenever the teacher believes that a review is in order or that the right hand and arm position can be improved by using this approach.

The Ready Hand Approach

Inner Game

The teacher is aware that the human hand automatically prepares itself for holding a tremendously large variety of objects in everyday life. He has made a special effort to observe the hand as it shapes itself to receive a book, a pitcher, a mint, a submarine sandwich, a baseball, and a sheet of paper. He has further observed that the hand, in such instances, always works as a unit and can anticipate the feel of an object before actually making contact with it.

Yet the teacher is aware that often something seems to go wrong when a student picks up a bow, perhaps because it seems so foreign to her. Through approaching the bow hold in this manner, the teacher consciously avoids the placement of one finger at a time, a method which appears to be contrary to nature.

If the teacher prefers, this approach can easily be adapted so that the student's hand is at the conventional location rather than the balance point.

The reader may wish to refer to the following mini-games:
26, *Finding the Balance Point*

Team Tactics

This approach can be used for all stringed instruments.

The Soft Landing Approach

Outer Game

The teacher shows the student how to use his left hand alone to balance the bow on a string. Though the shape of the hand is unimportant when performing this task, it must be on the stick directly above the place where the bow hair contacts the string and should push the stick down until it touches the hair. Also, the teacher should make certain that the bow is truly balanced and that it does not slant toward either of the two adjacent strings.

"Let's try this on the D string in the middle of the bow. . . . Good. Now imagine that there is an invisible bow suspended about eight or ten inches exactly above your real bow. Place your right hand in the conventional bow hold on the invisible bow.

"Now lower your right hand and arm as one unit to the real bow, making a soft landing. Your hand will feel like it's sinking into a bow stick made of rubber. When you release your left hand, you should still be able to keep the stick touching the hair at the place it contacts the string."

If the student is not able to do this the first time, the teacher should check to be sure that his bow hair is not too tight. Then she will encourage him to try again until he discovers the knack of channeling his arm weight and energy so that the stick will touch the hair.

"Good. Notice the alignment of your hand and arm and remember it. This is the way it should be when you play in the middle of the bow on the D string. It allows the energy to flow from your back through your spongy-feeling fingers to the top of the bow stick. In turn, the bow hair will sink into the flexible string. Take a photo. Click!

"Now, release the weight slightly so the stick no longer touches the hair as you start to pull your bow. Let's hear a beautiful tone."

After the student successfully accomplishes this, the teacher will guide him through the same process with the bow contacting the string at the frog, then at the tip. It is not possible, of course, for the stick to touch the hair at the extreme ends of the bow. The student will discover that, when he plays near the frog, his elbow will not only be closer to his body but will also point down, and his wrist will be curved.

When he plays at the tip, his elbow will be slightly higher and will be farther from his side, the line between his elbow and his hand will be direct and straight, and his hand and forearm will be pronated. Rather than using the term pronate, the teacher can say:

"Note that, when a cellist plays at the tip of her bow, she rotates her hand and wrist slightly as though she is going to look at her wristwatch. In fact, a good cellist who wears a watch on her right wrist should always be able to see its face at any position of the bow."

After several imaginary photos have been taken, the teacher will lead the student into drawing whole bows, both down and up.

"Stop drawing your bow when you reach the middle, and let's compare your position with the photo you took earlier. . . .

"This time stop your bow at the tip to compare your position with the photo you took after making a soft landing while the bow tip was held on the string."

Later this approach will be used on each string.

When to Use

1. Anytime, except at one of the earliest lessons, as an alternative approach.
2. Whenever the tone is weak.

Inner Game

The teacher believes that this approach is the best method to insure that the bow is properly balanced on the string and that the hand and arm alignment is good. She recognizes the value of positioning the bow on the string with the player's left hand before his right hand touches the bow. She also knows the effectiveness of using the invisible bow suspended above

the real bow because it makes the approach come from above.

The Soft Landing Approach is not suitable for one of the earliest lessons, except in the case of an adult beginner. However, it is extremely valuable for the student who has a small tone even though he has played the cello for some time.

The reader may wish to refer to the following mini-games:

Team Tactics

This approach is for cello students only.

CHECKPOINTS FOR HOME PRACTICE

Mini-games, or references to mini-games, may be used as effective checkpoints in home practice. Three lists of questions concerning the cello student's bow technique are given as examples of how mini-games can be compiled by the teacher, depending on the needs of the student. Obviously, list III was designed for a more advanced student. Similar lists can be devised for the other stringed instruments.

List I

1. Are the spaces between your fingers about the same as when you shake water off your hand?
2. Is your second finger opposite your thumb as though you have just picked a ripe red strawberry? Is your thumb not caved in?
3. Do your fingers cling to the bow as though it were smeared with honey?
4. When you prepare or change the position of your right hand, do you support the bow with your left hand?
5. When you play at the frog, does your arm form a road that goes around the bend and down a gentle slope?
6. When you play at the tip, does your arm form a road that goes straight from your elbow to the bow stick? Does the

road slant toward your body as though it is on an embankment?

7. Do the bow stick and the top of the bridge make a good set of railroad tracks?
8. Do you have a different arm level for each string?
9. Does your bow sink into the string as though it is in a deep groove?
10. Does the string continue to vibrate freely when your bow takes off like an airplane?

The reader may wish to refer to the following mini-games:
24, *The Dripping Wet Hand*
27, *Pick a Ripe Red Strawberry*
44, *Honey on the Bow Stick*
28, *The Bow Arm's Trusty Aide*
30, *Around the Bend and down a Gentle Slope*
32, *The Railroad Tracks*
35, *Comparing the Air Corridors*
43, *The Groovy String*
31, *The Airplane Stroke*
41, *Watch the Vibrations!*

List II

1. When you approach the bow hold from above, can you almost feel the stick before you actually touch it?
2. When you play at the tip, would a drop of oil on the back of your hand roll off on the thumb side?
3. When you play at the frog, does your elbow point down as though it is sinking into a soft

pillow? Is your thumb not caved in?

4. Does the magic dotted line formed by your base knuckles run almost parallel to the bow stick?
5. Is your hand and arm alignment exactly as though you are playing *YOU Are There!* —no matter what part of the bow you are playing in?
6. Are there no detours, hills, or valleys in the road from your elbow to your hand when you play at the tip?
7. When you play *Zip!* does your bow end up at the same spot on the string?
8. Does the design formed by your bow hair and the string look like a plus sign?
9. Can you make soft moon landings in any part of the bow?
10. Are the motions of your arm so free that you feel like a ballet dancer?

The reader may wish to refer to the following mini-games:
45, *A Drop of Oil*
49, *The Cushioned Elbow*
3, *The Magic Dotted Line*
46, *YOU Are There!*
30, *Around the Bend and down a Gentle Slope*
40, *Zip!*
32, *The Railroad Tracks*
61, *Moon Landings*
39, *The Ballet Dancer*
Also see
The Ready Hand Approach

List III

1. Are you holding the bow as though your hand has been dipped into wet glue?
2. Does your bow feel like an extension of your arm?
3. When you draw the bow, can you imagine that you are pulling it through a thick milkshake?
4. Can you make a tremolo in every part of the bow?
5. Are you good at skywriting with the tip of your bow?
6. Are your fingers flexible like the bristles of a paint brush in motion? Is your thumb also flexible?
7. Are you able to keep the bow in one lane?
8. Do your up-bows sound exactly like your down-bows?
9. Can you make good t sounds in every part of your bow?
10. Does your upper arm move as freely as the brakeman swinging his lantern?

The reader may wish to refer to the following mini-games:
34, *The Magic Wet Glue*
52, *A Magic Trick: Feeling through an Object*
62, *Pulling through a Milkshake*
37, *A Neat Sound Effect—the Tremolo*
59, *Skywriting*
79, *Painting*
51, *The Five-Lane Bowling Alley*
81, *Roping the Bow Arm*
66, *Can You Make a T Sound?*
47, *The Railroad Lantern*

8

Mini-Games for Building Left Hand Technique

The left hand is the acrobat of the team. Appearing to be in constant motion even in the slowest passages, it glides, soars, dives, dances, stretches, shakes, walks, runs, and leaps. The teacher's goal is to guide the student toward establishing a basic position and approach that will later allow him to perform every trick required to interpret the composer's music. The teacher has in mind not only the demands made by the existing literature but also the challenges that could be presented by composers as yet unborn.

The mini-games in this chapter may be used at the teacher's discretion to serve as a supplement to the student's method or solo book. They should be interspersed with the mini-games for building bow technique in chapter 7, with those for varied purposes in chapter 9, and with the teacher's own pedagogical devices. For the most part, they may be used in any order she deems appropriate. As always, the music itself must play the dominant role.

Approaches to establishing the left hand position by combining mini-games and checkpoints for home practice are included at the end of this chapter.

Throughout the text the words "tip" and "pad" have been used interchangeably to refer to the part of the finger which makes contact with the string. Since much depends on the shape of the student's hand, the passage being performed, and the individual's definition of the terms, this choice of words is left to the teacher's discretion.

The Cellist's Freeway
Mini-Game 82

Outer Game

When the student has assumed a playing posture, the teacher quickly traces a line with her index finger on the student's left arm. The line runs from the elbow to the base knuckles.

"Remember, the cellist's freeway has no hills, valleys, or winding curves. There is a direct line from the elbow to the base knuckles. Then, the fingers curve to the fingerboard."

When to Use

1. In one of the first lessons to help establish a good position of the left arm.
2. Whenever the teacher sees the student's left wrist protruding upward, his left wrist sinking inward, or his arm out of alignment with his hand.

Inner Game

The teacher knows the importance of establishing a position of the left arm and hand that allows the free flow of energy and weight from the player's back. If the wrist is arched so it looks like a hill, the fingers will move sluggishly. If the wrist sinks in so a valley is formed in the highway, the weight is directed to the underside of the wrist. The result is a loss of direct energy flow to the fingers, which can cause a grabbing, pushing, or clutching action; thus, the student's tone and technique can be adversely affected. In addition, the teacher is on the lookout for any kind of twist in the student's hand or arm which could be termed a curve in the road or a detour.

As an extension of this mini-game, the student can hold his bow against the highway to show that the road is straight and direct.

The reader may wish to refer to "Approaches to Establishing the Left Hand Position by Combining Mini-Games" before continuing.

Team Tactics

Though the position for holding the violin or the viola is different, there should always be a direct freeway between the player's left elbow and her base knuckles.

Airmail, Special Delivery
Mini-Game 83

Outer Game

Teacher: "Let's see how fast you can move your left hand. Touch the nut of the fingerboard. Now move your hand, with its curved fingers pointing down toward the fingerboard, as swiftly as possible through the air slightly above the strings and stop on the bridge. Now speed back to the nut, using the same direct route. Airmail, Special Delivery!"

When to Use

Frequently throughout the early training.

Inner Game

After this mini-game is repeated several times, the student's left elbow will gradually gravitate into a position that allows her hand to move quickly from one extreme location to the other. An additional benefit is that the speed forces her left arm and hand to work as a unit, thereby keeping a good alignment. Naturally the wrist must be flexible. This speedy action helps establish a feeling in the arm that will make shifting to and from thumb position much easier. It also prevents any tendency of the beginning cello student to twist her left shoulder back in order to watch her fingers. This bad habit is costly: it can cause back pains later, make shifting awkward, and weaken the tone by inhibiting the pulling action required in bowing.

Team Tactics

This mini-game is useful for violinists and violists, as well as cellists, in the early stages of learning to shift.

A Handful of Fruit
Mini-Game 84

Outer Game

Teacher: "Look, I brought some fruit today. Hold out your left hands."

The teacher proceeds to hand imaginary oranges, peaches, and plums to his students, carefully selecting the appropriate size for each student and identifying it.

"Don't eat it yet! See how you're holding the fruit. Your hand and fingers are gently curved just like a good left hand position for cello playing. Now let's see you place your hand on the fingerboard, keeping this in mind. Of course, your thumb will go under your second finger and will be straight."

When to Use

1. When introducing or reviewing the left hand position.
2. Anytime the teacher observes the student playing with straight, stiff fingers, resulting from the base knuckles being too far out from the cello neck, or with extremely flexed fingers, resulting from the base knuckles being so close to the cello neck that they are either caved in or completely flat.

Inner Game

The teacher recognizes that the term "curved fingers" does not help all students, because some curve only the first and second joints. This strained position does not produce the best tone, hampers dexterity, and can actually cramp the hand.

The mental image of the round fruit helps shape the whole hand and thumb as a unit. An added advantage is that most people tend to hold fruit with clinging fingers

—not grabbing fingers. The teacher can point this out if he chooses.

Team Tactics

This mini-game as stated applies primarily to the cello and the bass.

Rather than having a violinist or a violist stand on the sidelines, the teacher may wish to place an imaginary egg between the instrument neck and the left palm of the player.

The Leaning Index Finger
Mini-Game 85

Outer Game

Teacher: "A cellist's index finger is curved and tilts slightly so its second knuckle is closer to the scroll than its fingernail.

"That's why we call it the 'leaning index finger,' like a church tower in northern Italy is called the Leaning Tower of Pisa."

When to Use

1. Early in the training to help establish a good left hand position.
2. Whenever the teacher notices that the student's index finger does not have a slight tilt.

Inner Game

A slight tilt of the left index finger eases the hand into a position which allows a more beautiful vibrato and an agile technique. It

also makes it easier to adjust the spacing between the second and third fingers, thereby improving intonation.

By dramatizing this tilt with a name like that of the famous Italian tower, the teacher hopes the chances for her students' remembering it will be greater.

Note should be made that this outer game description does not apply to extended position. The reader may wish to refer to Mini-Game 116, *Stretching the Elastic Index Finger*, at this time.

Team Tactics

Though this mini-game is intended for cello students, the principle of a good left hand position being dependent on a well-shaped first finger is applicable to all stringed instruments.

What the Fingerboard Feels
Mini-Game 86

Outer Game

The teacher places his own left hand on the student's arm, allowing his strong but flexible fingers to sink into the flesh.

"This is how your fingerboard should feel if it were alive."

The teacher immediately follows this with a demonstration of what the fingerboard should *not* feel. He tightens his fingers and pushes down into the student's arm.

Mini-Game 86, *What the Fingerboard Feels*

When to Use

1. In one of the first lessons involving the left hand.
2. Anytime the teacher senses that the student is pushing down on the string with rigid, inflexible fingers.

Inner Game

This mini-game provides instant communication between teacher and student concerning the invisible flow of weight through the finger pads, which is a crucial factor in determining tone quality.

Team Tactics

Although all string students can be involved in this mini-game, it is most beneficial to cellists and bassists. Because of the thickness of their strings and the greater distance between the strings and the fingerboard, there is an instinctive tendency for these students to push down hard with their fingers, thereby tightening them. For this reason, it is especially important for cello and bass students to discover early the feeling of a flow of live energy from their backs down through their arms and fingers.

The Butterfly Tunnel
Mini-Game 87

Outer Game

Teacher: "Let's check your left hand position. Is there room for a butterfly to fly through the tunnel formed by your hand and the neck of your cello?"

When to Use

1. In one of the first lessons to help shape the left hand for playing in the neck positions.
2. Whenever the teacher notices that the student's left hand, when she plays in the neck positions, is collapsed, is held too near the neck of the cello, or is not rounded.

Inner Game

The mental image of the left hand forming a tunnel is effective and easy to remember. If the butterfly does not have enough space through which to fly, the student

will quickly adjust her hand and wrist position, thereby making it easy for her fingers to lift and drop from their base knuckles.

Team Tactics

While *The Butterfly Tunnel* is designed for cellists and bassists, the string teacher may wish to consider using an imaginary bumblebee to help check the left hand position of violin and viola students.

The Tender Cello Neck
Mini-Game 88

Outer Game

Teacher: "Treat the neck of your cello as you would like *your* neck to be treated. Don't squeeze or strangle it. Touch it tenderly as though it has feelings!"

When to Use

1. When the left hand position is introduced.
2. Throughout the training when the teacher perceives that the student's thumb is pushing up against the cello neck.

Inner Game

The teacher is aware that all students tend to push up with their thumbs unless they are constantly alerted to ward off this harmful inclination. A tight thumb restricts the power flow from the trunk through the arm as well as the maneuverability of the hand and fingers. It is also the surest way to create tension in the wrist.

The thumb, of course, is useful in offering a very slight counterpressure when balances are changed; however, it should never push tightly against the cello neck. Also, the thumb should not extend farther than the centerline of the neck.

Since tension is often not visible, the teacher's tapping on the student's thumb from time to time can both detect a problem and serve as a reminder. Should the student persist in squeezing the cello neck, the teacher may recommend that he practice for a limited time without touching the instrument with his thumb.

Team Tactics

The neck of any stringed instrument should be treated tenderly.

Four Mountain Peaks
Mini-Game 89

Outer Game

The teacher sits to the student's right.

"When I look at the profile of your left hand, I'd like to see four mountain peaks above your fingerboard. The tallest is formed by your second finger."

When to Use

1. During the first few weeks of lessons in order to help establish a good left hand position.
2. Anytime the teacher observes that the student is playing with straight fingers, with her left wrist so low that her fingers show very little curvature above the fingerboard, or with some fingers tucked under the neck of her cello.

Inner Game

The teacher recognizes that it is much more difficult to develop a facile technique when the hand hangs so low from the fingerboard that no mountain peaks are visible. The resulting faulty position can be the equivalent of the violinist's "pancake hand," since it prohibits finger action originating in the base knuckles, thus forcing the action into the first or second joints.

Care must be taken, however, that the student does not exaggerate by trying to make the mountain peaks too high when playing this mini-game because it becomes more difficult to spread the fingers apart. Neither extreme is desirable. It is very important that the fleshy tips of the fingers contact the string rather than the extreme tips, except in very fast passages.

Team Tactics

Although a well-shaped profile of the left hand is equally important in playing the violin or the viola, this description applies only to the cello and the bass.

Mini-Game 90, *The Buoy*

The Buoy can be adapted for bassists.

The Committee and Its Chairperson
Mini-Game 91

Outer Game

The teacher explains that the finger which determines the pitch of a note is called the playing finger and that the others, which rest on the string, are called the supporting fingers. For example:
When 4 is the playing finger, 1, 2, and 3 are the supporting fingers.
When 3 is the playing finger, 1 and 2 are the supporting fingers.
When 2 is the playing finger, 1 is the supporting finger.

"Let the weight of your arm flow through the playing finger only. You have a committee of fingers. The playing finger serves as its chairperson!"

When to Use

1. At the first lesson when notes are played by the second, third, or fourth finger.
2. Whenever the teacher senses that the student is distributing her weight through the supporting fingers or allowing her nonplaying fingers either to be raised high in the air or to be collapsed, possibly even on a different string.

Inner Game

The teacher recognizes that it is essential for the hand and fingers to feel as a unit, working together or independently as needed.

However, as the student advances, she will be made aware of two special circumstances:
1. When vibrato is used, the supporting fingers will be lifted slightly off the string. Yet the analogy of the committee will still be useful: the members will move with, never against, the chairperson.
2. When a fast passage is executed by the fingers, the chairperson's position will be abolished. The arm weight will be suspended, the balance will remain in the heel of the hand in line with the third or fourth finger, the tips of the fingers will contact the string, and

The Buoy
Mini-Game 90

Outer Game

Teacher: "Place your left hand in a good playing position on any string you choose. Fill the room with imaginary water until your left elbow is slightly submerged!

"Now, as your finger pads cling to the fingerboard, let your elbow bob around like a buoy until you find the location that makes your fingers feel the most clingy. . . . Good! Although your elbow will not bob around when you play, it will feel just as comfortable as it does right now. Let's hear you play this note."

The teacher will continue by guiding the students toward finding the imaginary water level suitable for playing on each string. It will be discovered that the elbow bobs best at a lower water level when the students play on the A string and at a higher level when they play on the C string.

When to Use

1. Early in the instruction in order to find the most effective height of the left elbow when the student plays on each string.
2. Anytime the teacher believes it will help alleviate any feeling of stiffness in the student's left arm and help him discover the sensation of clinginess in his fingers.

Inner Game

The teacher recognizes that frequently tension is created in the left hand because the student attempts to stretch his fingers across the strings to reach the locations required to produce the correct pitches. Often his arm and elbow will remain immobilized while he struggles to make his fingers longer.

It is important that the teacher call attention to the different arm levels required by each string and to the desirable feeling of looseness in the left elbow, which makes it possible to move gracefully from one level to another. Naturally, the thumb will pivot in its location under the second finger when changing strings; for example, it will favor the A string side of the neck when fingering C string passages.

the action of the fingers will be springy. The cellist's technique for playing fast passages is entirely different from that for slow passages, just as running requires a completely different body balance and leg action than walking.

By combining this mini-game with Mini-Game 92, *Using Your Head*, the power of the chairperson can quickly be determined. The reader may wish to refer to Mini-Game 124, *The Exer-Cycle*, at this time.

Team Tactics

This outer game can be applied to all stringed instruments.

Using Your Head
Mini-Game 92

Outer Game

Teacher: "In your home practice it can be helpful for you to shape your left hand on the top of your head, then lower it to the fingerboard. That's called using your head!"

When to Use

Anytime the teacher is trying to improve the position of the student's left hand and arm.

Inner Game

The teacher has observed that, when a person touches the top of her head, her hand and arm are usually well aligned. Yet a student will often try to play a cello with his left wrist arched out, caved in, or twisted. This mini-game serves as a readily available checkpoint for home practice.

Using Your Head can be combined effectively with Mini-Game 91, *The Committee and Its Chairperson*. The player's scalp can quickly determine if the chairperson carries more weight than the other members of the committee.

Team Tactics

Violin and viola students can take a breather—using the head in this manner is applicable only to cellists and some seated bassists.

Mini-Game 91, The Committee and Its Chairperson

The Siren
Mini-Game 93

Outer Game

The teacher shows the student how to slide her left hand on her first, second, and third finger pads gently up and down the entire length of the fingerboard with a glissando effect resembling a siren. No pitches are specified.

"Slide smoothly as though the string has been soaked in olive oil. You can't go wrong in this mini-game if your hand retains its good form and you don't try to push the string down. Let your thumb be straight and its side laid across two strings as it rides with your hand into the upper registers. Glide and soar like a bird in the sky or a fish in the ocean!"

When to Use

1. Soon after introducing the position of the left arm and hand.
2. Throughout the early training to emphasize freedom in motion and to sample an action important in advanced left hand technique.
3. Whenever the teacher perceives that the student is holding her left arm in a position which could make shifting to the upper registers difficult or is pushing her thumb tightly against the cello neck.

Inner Game

This mini-game is perhaps the most vital of all 165 in this book. Because shifting the left hand up and down the fingerboard is one of the most important and most characteristic motions in cello playing, the wise teacher introduces it early.

Since no pitches are specified and this mini-game is great fun, with the added bonus of marvelous sound effects, the hand can glide freely without the slightest need for caution. Designated pitches of the top and bottom notes can be added later at the instructor's discretion as an effective and exciting ear training game.

The teacher should watch carefully to be sure that the student's left shoulder does not twist back as his hand returns to the first or the second position. If it does, a readjustment of the placement of the cello may be necessary. See Mini-Game 13, *The Chipmunk*.

Also, the teacher should make sure that, while his hand is in one of the first four positions, the student can add his fourth finger easily without having to change the alignment of his arm and hand. Only three fingers were specified in *The Siren* so the hand shape in the fifth position and higher would be more nearly like that actually used in music making. The fourth finger is rarely used in these registers since the closer spacing of intervals permits a whole step to be played between any two adjacent fingers and since it is natural for the fingers to point slightly toward the bridge in these positions.

The Siren is an indispensable aid to the beginning game teacher in achieving the immediate goal of establishing the habit of making tension-free motions, as presented in chapter 2 and described in greater detail in chapter 10. The motions should be made leisurely, with an emphasis on fluidity and the sensation that the forearm provides the transportation for the hand.

Team Tactics

This mini-game as described is for cello and bass students only. However, if the statement about thumb placement is eliminated and all four fingers are used, the outer game can also help violin and viola students. The teacher may prefer, however, that these students move only through the first five positions in the initial playing of *The Siren*. In the upper registers the bassist's thumb will slide on only one string.

The Expanding Telescope
Mini-Game 94

Outer Game

Teacher: "Using both hands, form a telescope so you can see that imaginary deer in the distance. . . . Now expand your hands so your telescope gives you a bigger picture."

When the distance between the pad of the rounded second finger and the thumb is the same as that between the top of the fingerboard and the underside of the cello neck, the teacher will say:

"Stop! Your left hand is in a perfect position for cello playing. Try playing your piece again, keeping this same shape. Naturally you will adjust the space between your fingers in order to play in tune."

When to Use

Anytime the teacher notices that, when she plays in the neck positions, the student's left hand is collapsed, held too near the neck of the cello, not rounded, or not in good alignment with her arm.

Inner Game

Viewing wildlife through an imaginary telescope is appealing to most children. The teacher's goal is to capitalize on an activity already familiar to his students and relate it to cello playing.

Team Tactics

The Expanding Telescope as described is for cello and bass students only. However, the principle of holding the left arm in position, making a fist, then gradually opening the fingers to form a tube-shaped tunnel can also be applied to the violin and the viola. The thumb must be allowed to find its natural position, which is not necessarily opposite the second finger.

The Rubber Fingerboard
Mini-Game 95

Outer Game

Teacher: "Let your fingers sink into the fingerboard as though it is made of rubber."

When to Use

Anytime the teacher senses that the student's finger joints are rigid or that the student is pushing her fingers down rather than allowing them to sink into the fingerboard.

Inner Game

The teacher recognizes that hard, inflexible fingers never produce a tone of good quality and cause tension that restricts technique. Yet, if he advises the student to make her fingers looser, there is a great possibility that there will not be enough weight in the playing finger. The mental image of the finger pads sinking into rubber helps produce the desired combination of strength and flexibility.

Team Tactics

This mini-game is applicable to all stringed instruments but is most useful with the cellists.

A Precision Diving Team
Mini-Game 96

Outer Game

The teacher points out that, when open strings are used, the fingers of the left hand should hover over the string on which the forthcoming notes will be played.

"When you bow an open string, your fingers should point down toward the string like a precision team of four divers aiming for the water. They are all about the same distance above the water."

When to Use

1. During the first few months of lessons to help establish a good left hand position.
2. Whenever the teacher notices that the student's fingers point up, are straight, do not hover above the string to be used for the forthcoming notes, or are slanted so they resemble a violinist's left hand position.

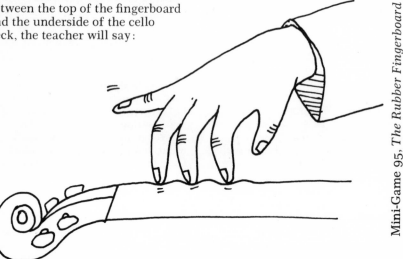

Mini-Game 95, *The Rubber Fingerboard*

Inner Game

The teacher is aware that all beginning students have a tendency to point their fingers up to the sky when playing open strings. This sometimes happens because the hand is positioned so low in relation to the fingerboard that it is the only way the student can clear the string. Should this appear to be the problem, *The Indian War Dance Approach*, toward the end of this chapter, is recommended to help position the hand so the fingers are able to spring up from the base knuckles and remain in a curved shape.

This mini-game helps the student in a heterogeneous class check his left hand to make sure he has not adopted a position resembling that of a violinist. If he has, the first diver (his first finger) will appear considerably closer to the water than the fourth. Thus, the mental image of this precision team of divers approaching the water will help correct this faulty position. Care should be taken, however, that the fingers do not become vertical; the landing should be on the fleshy tips—not the extreme tips—of the fingers unless fast technique is involved.

If the student has difficulty with this mini-game, the teacher should check to be sure his left shoulder is not twisted backward. See Mini-Game 18, *The Puppet Dance*, and Mini-Game 13, *The Chipmunk*.

Team Tactics

A Precision Diving Team can be played by all string students. Although the slant of the fingers is different for the violin or the viola, the analogy presented in the outer game is still applicable.

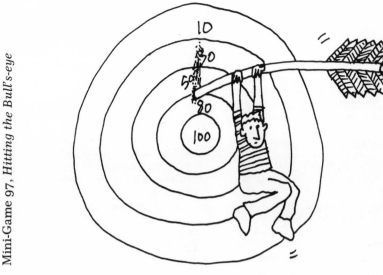

Mini-Game 97, *Hitting the Bull's-eye*

Hitting the Bull's-eye
Mini-Game 97

Outer Game

"A truly beautiful note sounds perfectly on pitch from the instant it starts. This, of course, means we must aim the finger so it lands on exactly the right spot on the string. Let's watch an archer practice hitting his target."

The teacher reaches for an imaginary bow and arrow.

"Watch him pose his bow and release the arrow. It missed! What does he do?"

The teacher strides across the room to an invisible target, grabs the arrow, and slides it into the bull's-eye.

"Why are you laughing, Delta and Tinka? The archer is correcting his error!"

After the students discuss the proper way to practice hitting a target, the teacher summarizes:

"If an archer corrected his error by sliding his arrow from the incorrect spot to the correct spot, his score would never improve! The real pro makes note of the size and direction of his error, then reaims and reshoots the arrow. He practices until he knows exactly where to aim.

"Naturally we will not stop the music and reshoot our fingers while performing in public or with an ensemble. Instead we will make the necessary pitch adjustments by sliding our fingers on the string. But, in our home practice, let's follow the example of the prize-winning archer!"

When to Use

Whenever the teacher wants to stress good intonation, clean technique, and effective practice habits.

Inner Game

The teacher recognizes that the student with the most sensitive mental ear is the one most prone to slide her fingers around on the string until she finds the correct pitch. Although the ability to adjust intonation through horizontal finger motion is essential to fine string playing, its overuse deters the development of a clean technique.

Team Tactics

Hitting the Bull's-eye is for all string instrumentalists.

Mini-Game 96,
A Precision Diving Team

The Arch of a Rainbow
Mini-Game 98

Outer Game

Teacher: "Allow your left hand and fingers to arch over the fingerboard when you play on the lower strings. Think of the shape of a beautiful rainbow!"

When to Use

1. Anytime the teacher observes that the student's left hand is positioned extremely low, with the thumb almost vertical, or is in a cramped position with the base knuckles unusually close to the cello neck.
2. Whenever the teacher notices that the student is stretching his fingers across to the lower strings.

Inner Game

The teacher knows that this mental image is appealing to almost everyone and that it helps the left hand assume a good rounded shape. Thus, there is a reasonable assurance that the finger action required by fast technique will originate from the base knuckles. Also, in this position, the chances are greater that in slow technique the weight will be channeled through the arm and hand into the finger pads. If the arch is positioned too high, however, the spread of the fingers is restricted and faulty intonation will result.

Team Tactics

The arch of the left hand is important for any instrument requiring finger dexterity.

Cooked Macaroni
Mini-Game 99

Outer Game

Teacher: "Let's hear you play a note with your fourth finger. Allow all the weight to flow through your arm and through your fourth finger as its pad sinks into the fingerboard. Your other three fingers will touch the same string but will feel like cooked macaroni. In fact, if the fingerboard had feeling, it would be aware only of your fourth finger.

"While you play, I'll tap your other fingers lightly to see if they remind me of cooked macaroni."

This mini-game will be repeated, allowing each finger to take its turn in assuming the role of the playing finger.

When to Use

1. Early in the training.
2. Anytime the teacher senses stiffness or tension in a nonplaying finger. It is especially important for the student to gain this sensation before vibrato is introduced.

Inner Game

It is vital for the student to establish from the beginning the habit of relaxing the fingers which do not determine the pitch of the note so that all of the weight and energy can flow through the playing finger only.

Care should be taken that the nonplaying fingers retain their form even though they will feel as nonenergetic as cooked macaroni.

Team Tactics

Cooked Macaroni is for all string students except bassists.

Wiping the String
Mini-Game 100

Outer Game

Teacher: "When practicing, it's helpful to stop periodically and wipe one of your cello strings with your finger pads. Let them move up and down the entire length of the fingerboard in a sensitive, graceful manner. The string will feel like silk under your fingers."

When to Use

1. Frequently throughout the early training.
2. Whenever the teacher observes that the student shifts with awkward, jerky motions, pushes her thumb tightly against the cello neck, or holds her arm so it will be difficult to move to the upper registers.

Inner Game

The teacher knows that the act of wiping is a graceful motion familiar to all people. By interspersing this mini-game throughout early lessons and home practice, the student is sampling the technique of shifting, which plays a prominent role in advanced cello playing. As an alternative, the term "caress" can be an effective substitute for "wipe."

Team Tactics

String wiping benefits all string students.

Spring Checkup
Mini-Game 101

Outer Game

The student places his left hand in a good playing position.

Teacher: "Imagine that there's a wire coil spring in each joint of your hand and arm. I'm going to tug gently back on your elbow as though I'm trying to pull your hand off the fingerboard. It won't come off, however, because of that wonderful suction between the finger pad of your playing finger and the fingerboard. Instead, the springs will uncoil. Allow your thumb to leave its place on the neck while I do this. . . ."

After the teacher has pulled on the student's arm so that his fingers are extended, she adds:

"Now watch when I release your arm. All the coils will contract and your hand and arm will spring back to its good position! It will seem almost like the fingerboard is a magnet."

When to Use

1. Frequently during the first few months of study.
2. Anytime the teacher perceives that the student's fingers are rigid; the student has not discovered the feeling of suction between his finger pads and the fingerboard; or the student's wrist is tight.

Inner Game

The primary goal of this mini-game is to check the position, flexibility, weight, and balance of the student's left hand and arm. The mini-game also conveys an image which will help him acquire the feeling of springs in his joints and suction in his finger pads.

If the student's hand slips off the fingerboard when his teacher tugs gently on his arm, he usually will quickly make the necessary adjustments, thereby discovering the important concept of strength and flexibility which is the basis for a good left hand technique. In home practice the student's right hand can take over the teacher's role of tugging on the left arm.

Team Tactics

Though the principle of imagining springs in each joint is applicable to all stringed instruments, this tugging action to be executed by the teacher as a checkup is best suited to cello and possibly string bass students.

Mini-Game 102,
Four Birds on a Fence

Four Birds on a Fence
Mini-Game 102

Outer Game

Teacher: "While I sit here to your right, show me a good left hand profile. I'd like to see four birds sitting on a fence."

When to Use

Whenever the teacher observes the student holding her left hand so low in relation to the fingerboard that it shows very little profile or in a tilted position resembling that of a violinist.

Inner Game

A young cello student taught by a violinist or surrounded by violin students in a heterogeneous class

frequently has the tendency to shape her left hand like that of a violinist.

Though a *slight* slant of the fingers is not harmful, the teacher should be particularly careful that the hand does not turn so the line formed by the base knuckles points in toward the nut rather than running in almost the same direction as the strings.

A hand position that resembles that of a violinist makes accurate intonation impossible because it cramps the spacing of the fingers, produces a weak tone by cutting off the power line from the trunk through the elbow, and reduces all possibility of the development of a beautiful free vibrato.

Care, of course, must be taken that the student does not overcompensate by making his hand

alignment very square or by placing his fingers in a vertical position, since either of these positions limits the ability of the fingers to spread apart.

Team Tactics

This is a good time for violin and viola students to take a break.

Suction Fingers
Mini-Game 103

Outer Game

The teacher guides her students in a discussion of the human hand and its incredible ability to form many different shapes and to do a great variety of things. A number of suitable props can easily be provided.

Gradually it is discovered that, in addition to all its other attributes, the hand can assume a suctionlike quality when holding such commonplace objects as a drinking glass, a book, or a broom handle. While one student holds a water tumbler with his suction fingers, the other students will demonstrate that removing it is unexpectedly difficult. However, if the glass is held by hard, rigid fingers, its removal is markedly easier.

The teacher explains that a fine cellist has this same feeling of suction or clinginess in her fingers when she holds a bow or makes contact with the fingerboard. The students experiment with applying this phenomenon to their cello playing.

When to Use

1. During the first few weeks of instruction.
2. Anytime the teacher senses that a student is grabbing or pushing with his fingers.

Inner Game

The string teacher's goal is to make good use of the natural capabilities of the human hand. She knows, however, that often a student will approach a bow stick or a fingerboard in a completely foreign manner unless special care is taken.

Team Tactics

This mini-game is for the entire string class.

The Eight-Fingered Hand
Mini-Game 104

Outer Game

The teacher shows the student how to interlace her fingers so her hands form a dome shape resembling an Eskimo's igloo. The tips of the fingers of one hand will touch the webs of skin between the base knuckles of the other hand.

"Now you have an eight-fingered hand! Remove your right hand and look at the spacing of the fingers of your left hand. If you should have trouble spreading your fingers far enough apart in your home practice, think of your eight-fingered hand! Just insert some imaginary fingers."

When to Use

1. During the first few weeks of instruction when establishing a good hand position for playing in first position.
2. Whenever the student fails to spread her fingers far enough apart for good intonation.

Inner Game

The teacher is aware that some students have difficulty spreading their fingers far enough apart for cello playing and that this problem can become worse if their attention is focused on their fingertips. However, if one thinks of putting space between the base knuckles, the whole hand seems to expand. By interlacing the fingers, the emphasis is immediately taken away from the ends of the fingers.

Naturally, with the variety of hand sizes and the disparity of fingerboard lengths, good intonation is dependent on the guidance of the mental ear. This mini-game simply helps the student expand her hand from its center by providing the image of inserted fingers. If she continues to have difficulty, the teacher should check to be sure that her hand is not too square in its placement on the fingerboard. With even the slightest pulling back of the left wrist toward the player's shoulder, the spacing between the second and third fingers becomes much easier to control. The teacher should also check to be sure that the student's base knuckles are not too high in relation to the edge of the fingerboard.

Since the spacing of the fingers in this mini-game does not apply to extended position, the reader may wish to refer to Mini-Game 116, *Stretching the Elastic Index Finger*, at this time.

Team Tactics

Though *The Eight-Fingered Hand* is intended for cello students because of the distances involved between half steps, the principle of expanding the hand from its center rather than concentrating on the fingertips is applicable to other instruments.

The Helicopters
Mini-Game 105

Outer Game

Teacher: "When you play an open string, imagine that your fingers are four helicopters hovering over the string to be used in the following notes. All four should be at about the same altitude and should be ready to land in a split second by simply dropping to the fingerboard."

When to Use

1. During the first lessons involving the left hand.
2. Anytime the teacher notes that, when an open string is played, the student's fingers are pointing up to the sky, are not above the string of the forthcoming notes, or are straight rather than curved.

Inner Game

The teacher recognizes that good intonation is dependent on the hand retaining its form even while open strings are played. If the student continually lifts his fingers off the fingerboard by straightening them, even after playing this mini-game, the teacher should check to be sure that his base knuckles are not too low in relation to the cello neck. In such a case, a review using *The Indian War Dance Approach*, described toward the end of this chapter, is recommended.

Team Tactics

The Helicopters as described in the outer game is applicable to the violin and viola as well as cello and string bass.

Getting the Hang of It
Mini-Game 106

Outer Game

Teacher: "Think of your left arm as hanging on a hook! Your playing finger and your hand form the hook. Be sure to keep your playing finger curved. Allow your elbow to sag a little bit. . . .

"There! You're getting the hang of it!"

When to Use

When the teacher observes the student holding her left elbow in an extremely high and awkward position.

Inner Game

The teacher knows that, in addition to being awkward, an extremely high elbow often indicates the presence of tension. The word "hang" signals an immediate release, and the muscles will become more relaxed.

In playing this mini-game, care must be taken that the left hand does not lose its form. The fingers should still arch over the fingerboard while the arm is hanging.

See Mini-Game 98, *The Arch of a Rainbow*. Also, the student should be reminded that the level of her elbow will vary slightly, depending on which string is being used. See Mini-Game 117, *The Floating Elbow*.

Team Tactics

This mini-game is for cellists and, possibly, bass players who are seated.

The Zombies
Mini-Game 107

Outer Game

Teacher: "Remember that weight should flow through your playing finger *only*, although the others will be on the string. These others, which we call supporting fingers, will just sit on the string like featherweight zombies."

When to Use

Anytime the teacher perceives that there is weight in any finger other than the finger which determines the pitch.

Inner Game

The teacher knows that the development of a beautiful vibrato in later lessons will depend on the hand and arm being perfectly balanced on the playing finger and that the student's discovery of this concept of balance early in his training will help him enormously. Of course, when the student uses vibrato, his supporting fingers will not be required to stay down on the string. However, traditionally in the early training, the supporting fingers remain on the string to insure that the hand is well shaped and that intonation is accurate.

Team Tactics

This outer game applies to all stringed instruments except bass.

Trapping the Flea
Mini-Game 108

Outer Game

Teacher: "See that little flea on your fingerboard? Trap it with a finger before it gets away!"

When to Use

When the teacher wishes to emphasize the rapid finger action required in the playing of fast passages.

Inner Game

The teacher has observed that children on the playground constantly demonstrate their ability to move quickly. However, often the same youngsters exhibit labored, even sluggish motions in a music class. Catching an imaginary flea before it jumps can motivate any child to move swiftly!

Team Tactics

This mini-game is applicable to all musical instruments requiring finger dexterity.

The Red-Hot Fingerboard
Mini-Game 109

Outer Game

Teacher: "Let's pretend that your fingerboard is so hot that, if water were splashed on it, you would hear it sizzle! With your left hand in a good position, drop your fingers on this hot surface!"

Naturally the student will touch her fingerboard only momentarily and will then flip her fingers off it. If her hand position is correct, the motion should come from her base knuckles. If not, the teacher will guide her in making the necessary adjustment.

"When a string player performs fast passages, the springing action of his fingers is as important as dropping them. Let's practice playing these fast notes. . . ."

When to Use

Anytime the teacher wishes to emphasize the springing action of the fingers, especially as required by fast descending passages.

Inner Game

The teacher's goal is to relate the springing action of the fingers, an essential left hand technique, to an experience with which the student is familiar.

Team Tactics

All music students who play instruments that require finger dexterity can benefit from this mini-game.

The Soft Elastic Thumb
Mini-Game 110

Outer Game

Teacher: "Think of your left thumb as being made of soft elastic as it gently touches the cello neck. Let's see all the different directions in which you can move your hand and fingers above the fingerboard! Show me how pliable your thumb is! Use it as a pivot while you move your hand in large circular motions."

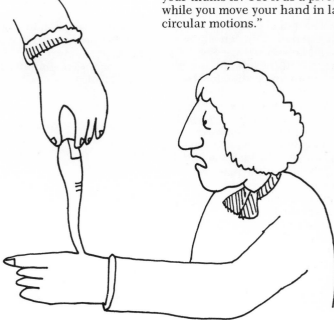

Mini-Game 110, *The Soft Elastic Thumb*

When to Use

Whenever the teacher senses that the student's thumb is stiff or tight.

Inner Game

The teacher recognizes that, through playing this mini-game, the student is establishing the habit of making the tension-free motions essential to good left hand technique and tone production.

Team Tactics

Every member of the string class can play this mini-game.

A Guessing Game
Mini-Game 111

Outer Game

While a student silently fingers a scale in first position, the teacher blocks his classmates' view of his left hand with a sheet of paper.

"Watch Mike's left elbow as it gently floats from one level to another. Steve, is he playing an ascending or a descending scale?"

When to Use

Anytime the teacher believes the students would benefit from being made more conscious of the slight change in height of the left elbow when crossing strings.

Inner Game

The teacher wishes to call attention not only to the changing left arm levels but also to the gentle floating action of the left elbow as the hand crosses strings. She knows that, if the left arm is not in the optimum position for the string being played on, the student will tend to exert extra finger pressure in order to hold down the string. Pushing, grabbing, or squeezing actions should be avoided since they cause tension which adversely affects the tone and technique.

This mini-game has a twofold effect: the student must demonstrate the action well in order to give his classmates a fair chance, and those guessing must know that the left elbow moves down slightly as the scale ascends to the upper

strings and up slightly as the scale descends to the lower strings.

Team Tactics

A *Guessing Game* is designed primarily for cello and bass students. Although the floating action of the elbow is also applicable to the violin and the viola, the change in level is much less perceptible.

Fingerboard Geography
Mini-Game 112

Outer Game

Teacher: "Today let's explore the geography of your cello's fingerboard! Let's search for all the places where you can find D's. Explore every string."

When to Use

Whenever the teacher wishes to help his students become more familiar with the fingerboard and better understand the relationship between string length and pitch.

Inner Game

This mini-game is an excellent ear training study. In addition, it helps the student discover for herself the fingerboard's geography and the principle that a note is the same even if it is played on a different string or with a different finger. It also aids in developing quick reflexes in the adjustment of intonation so the student does not have to pause before deciding in which direction to move her hand in order to raise or lower the pitch.

Explorations for pitches other than D, of course, will follow.

Team Tactics

It is important for every string instrumentalist to be thoroughly familiar with the geography of her fingerboard.

Meat of the Finger
Mini-Game 113

Outer Game

Teacher: "Try playing this passage using the meat of your fin-

gers. That's where you will find your most beautiful tone!"

When to Use

Anytime the teacher believes the student's playing of a particular passage will improve if he shapes his fingers so that more flesh contacts the string.

Inner Game

The purpose of this mini-game is to describe the fleshy tips of the fingers in a term not easily forgotten. Except in very fast passages, which are best executed by using the extreme tips of the fingers, most cellists find their warmest tones are produced when their finger meat spreads out over the string while their fingers retain their curved shape.

Team Tactics

This mini-game is primarily intended for cello and bass students.

All Fingers on Deck!
Mini-Game 114

Outer Game

Teacher: "Be careful that none of your fingers are below deck asleep! All fine cellists keep their fingers ready to spring into action when needed. If some are tucked below the fingerboard, they are like sailors asleep in their bunks below deck."

When to Use

When the teacher observes a student holding some fingers below the fingerboard while playing with others.

Inner Game

The teacher knows that almost all children have an inclination to adopt this undesirable habit of tucking some fingers under the fingerboard unless care is taken to avoid it. She further recognizes that all children seek comfort and that this faulty position must be very comfortable indeed for the tendency to be so widespread.

In addition to calling out "All fingers on deck!" when appropri-

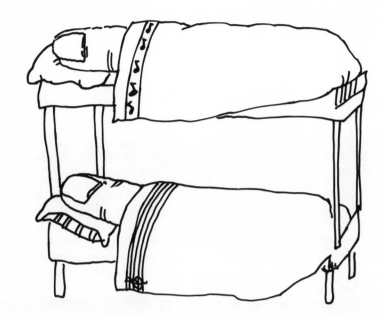

ate, it is recommended that the teacher assign some fast finger exercises so there is no time for a finger to go below deck.

Team Tactics

This mini-game was designed to solve a problem which primarily occurs with cello and bass students.

The Space Platform
Mini-Game 115

Outer Game

Teacher: "When you're playing an open string, rest your fingertips on an imaginary space platform suspended an inch or so directly above the string on which you will play the forthcoming notes.

"Rather than pulling your fingers up and/or over to this rest station, let your hand and fingers give a little flip, as though you are splashing water off the back of your hand. Your fingers will bounce back to the space platform and feel completely nonenergetic."

When to Use

1. After the playing position is well established and the left hand technique is beginning to develop.

2. Anytime the teacher notices that the student's hand is not retaining a good form while an open string is being played, has a rigid, clawlike appearance while an open string is being played, looks sluggish when executing the lifting action, or is not held above the forthcoming notes while an open string is being played.

Inner Game

The teacher recognizes that the image of the fingers resting on a space platform helps the student retain a good playing form yet at the same time gain a feeling of relaxation. It is important to stress that the space platform is above the string on which the forthcoming notes are found and that the actions of lifting the fingers and moving them to this rest station should be consolidated into one motion. However, the flips and their rebounds must first be practiced above each individual string, following notes played on that string; the consolidation of flipping and moving to a different space platform can easily be made after the student has discovered the flipping sensation. At first there will be a tendency to drop the fingers back to the string in the rebound action rather than to the space platform.

Team Tactics

All string students can play this mini-game.

Stretching the Elastic Index Finger
Mini-Game 116

Outer Game

Teacher: "When the space between your first and second fingers is expanded to a whole step instead of a half step, it is called the left hand extension or the extended position. We do this by stretching the index finger backward, making it feel almost like elastic. I'll show you how!

"Place your hand lightly in first position so your fourth finger will sound D on the A string. Holding your upper fingers in their usual places, lift up your first finger. As you do this, allow its base knuckle to sink in and that side of your hand and wrist to rotate very slightly as though you plan to look at your wristwatch. Your index finger will make a small arc in the air over an imaginary wad of chewing gum which is stuck on your fingerboard, then drop on B♭. Good!

"Now let's hear you play the first three notes of 'Three Blind Mice.' The fingering is 4, 2, 1 in this new spacing. Your thumb will remain under your second finger."

After the student is able to do this with ease, the teacher will have him shift his arm and hand so the fourth finger plays D♯, and the opening of the song will be repeated. Then, his arm and hand will be shifted again so the fourth finger plays E, etc.

When to Use

When introducing the extended position, which involves a major third between the first and the fourth fingers on the same string.

Inner Game

There are two kinds of spacing in the first through the fourth positions on the cello:

1. A half step between each adjacent finger, with the distance between the first and the fourth fin-

gers being a minor third when the cellist plays on one string.

2. A whole step between the first and the second fingers, a half step between the second and the third, and a half step between the third and the fourth; thus, the interval between the first and the fourth fingers, when the cellist plays on the same string, is a major third.

The teacher's goal in this mini-game is to help the student learn how to execute the second kind of spacing, commonly referred to as an extension or an extended position. It should be executed by stretching the index finger backward—never by extending the second, third, and fourth fingers forward. The student must avoid the latter, which causes great tension in the hand, by shifting his forearm so it always remains aligned with his fourth finger. The imaginary wad of chewing gum helps the student rotate his index finger in the air, because no one wants to touch the gum! Without this lifting and rotating motion, tension can also be created.

Since the procedure of achieving this desired hand position is more complicated when an ascending scale passage is played, such a passage should be delayed until the student feels comfortable with this mini-game. However, the reader may wish to refer to Mini-Game 125, *The Sliding Thumb*, at this time.

Team Tactics

Stretching the Elastic Index Finger is for cellists only.

The Floating Elbow
Mini-Game 117

Outer Game

Teacher: "Let's pantomime the action of your left hand and arm in an imaginary first position piece that has many string crossings. With only your thumb lightly touching the neck of your cello, let your fingers walk or run from one imaginary string to another. Your hand will float an inch or so above the fingerboard, moving across the strings with your fingers. In this way the weight focused through your finger pads will always drop from above.

"To accomplish this, your elbow will also move. It will float up and down, being higher when you play on the C string than on the A string."

When to Use

1. As a preparatory exercise for a piece involving many string crossings.
2. Anytime the teacher observes that the student is trying to cross strings with her fingers only (exception: frequently in broken chord passages, it is advisable for the hand to remain in one position as though a double stop were being played) or the student moves her left arm in a jerky manner when crossing strings.

Inner Game

The teacher recognizes the importance of the left hand and arm being in the optimum position for the weight to drop through the fingers. He knows that if this position is not obtained the student will tighten her fingers in her effort to push the string down. This latter action, of course, can be harmful and will reduce the chances of developing a beautiful vibrato later.

If the student does not acquire this feeling of the floating elbow immediately, the teacher should check the finger joints to be sure they are flexible. If even one finger joint is rigid, the floating action of the arm will be hampered. Also, he should check to be sure the student's thumb is not tight and is able to pivot freely.

Team Tactics

Floating elbows are especially important to cellists and bassists.

The Thumb Rail
Mini-Game 118

Outer Game

The teacher shows the student how to make a gentle fist by rolling up his four fingers while his thumb sticks straight out.

"Now place the side of your thumb on two strings and let it ride up and down the length of the fingerboard. It will feel like it has

two grooves which are riding on the rails formed by the strings. The weight of your arm will flow through the side of your thumb. Be sure to keep your fingers from touching the strings. Your base knuckles will point up and out. This will help you play well in thumb position."

When to Use

1. As a first step in preparing for thumb position study.
2. Whenever the teacher notes that the student's hand caves in when he plays in thumb position.

Inner Game

The teacher's goal is to strengthen the hand in preparation for thumb position study. She is aware of the common tendency for the hand to collapse when the arm weight rests on the thumb, thereby hampering the facility of the fingers.

Team Tactics

This mini-game is exclusively for cellists and bassists; however, only one string is used on the bass.

Shifting Tricks
Mini-Game 119

Outer Game

Teacher: "Knowing several tricks can help you shift from one note to another on the same string or on different strings. I look on it as taking a trip from one city to another. Here are several ways to make the trip easier:

"1. Know exactly where you are before you start out on your trip. Be able to say the letter name of the first note, the finger with which you play it, and its position (first, second, etc.).

"2. Know your final destination. Be able to say the letter name of the second note, the finger with which you play it, and its position. You should be able to play it perfectly in pitch when approaching it from ten to fifteen inches above the fingerboard as an isolated note.

"3. Know your mode of transportation. On which finger or fingers do you travel?

"4. Practice going very slowly from the first note to the second and back, consciously measuring the distance between the two locations. Remember the feeling in your arm and hand, especially in the angle of your elbow.

"5. Practice moving on the string so smoothly that it feels like you're wiping a silken string. Your arm weight will be suspended during the trip.

"6. But, most important of all, make a conscious effort to sing silently in your mental ear the pitch of the second note before starting your journey. This will take you directly to the note, almost like radar guides a 747 to its destination!"

When to Use

When introducing or reviewing shifting.

Inner Game

This mini-game stresses the basic principles of shifting, a very important technique in string playing. It should be preceded by Mini-Game 93, *The Siren*.

Team Tactics

These six tricks for shifting are to be shared with violin, viola, and string bass students.

Amtrak Tunnel
Mini-Game 120

Outer Game

Teacher: "When playing in thumb position, be sure your hand and fingers form a nice arch. I think of an Amtrak railroad tunnel through a mountain."

When to Use

1. When introducing thumb position.
2. Anytime the teacher observes the student's hand collapsed when he plays in thumb position.

Inner Game

The teacher recognizes that this arched hand shape is important when the student plays in thumb position and that his fingers should be more vertical than when he plays in the neck positions. If the

Amtrak tunnel repeatedly collapses, more time should be spent practicing Mini-Game 118, *The Thumb Rail*, in order to build up strength.

Later this mini-game can be effectively combined with pantomiming fast finger action in the air, similar to that described in Mini-Game 124, *The Exer-Cycle*. However, this combination should not be attempted before strength is well developed in the student's left thumb and hand. Moreover, only the first, second, and third fingers will participate since the fourth finger is seldom used in thumb position.

Team Tactics

The *Amtrak Tunnel* is primarily for cellists.

Thrilling Trills
Mini-Game 121

Outer Game

The teacher guides the student in learning how to execute fast trills by lifting and dropping her fingers, practicing first on the upper left bout of the cello.

"Before starting a trill, shape your fingers on the string so the weight flows through the finger which will play the top note. Then lift and drop that finger without changing the balance point in your hand. Of course, when playing some whole step trills, you will lift and drop a pair of fingers as a single unit. Concentrate on the lifting action, not the dropping action, so your fingers can move like lightning!"

Mini-Game 120, *Amtrak Tunnel*

When to Use

1. As a preparatory exercise for a piece involving fast finger dexterity or as a sample of a more advanced technique.
2. Anytime the teacher wishes to improve the student's fast technique.

Inner Game

The teacher recognizes that trills are excellent practice for developing fast technique. They are not only fun to play but also have the advantage of being an example of fast technique that can be introduced before note reading is well established. Thus, the student is able to discover the feeling in her hand and fingers which she will often use later when playing more advanced literature; the successful playing of rapid trills in the early stages of training helps insure the workability of her left hand position. If the student concentrates on keeping her hand balanced in one spot and on the lifting action of the fingers from the base knuckles rather than on the dropping action, she should be able to gain considerable speed. *Thrilling Trills* should be performed on all parts of the fingerboard.

Team Tactics

Although this description is primarily intended for teaching cello students, all string students can benefit from playing trills early in their training.

The Blind Man's Touch
Mini-Game 122

Outer Game

Teacher: "When you practice, consciously measure the distance between your fingers as required by the notes in the passage. Imagine a blind man dialing a telephone or using the type of telephone with the little singing push buttons. You can be sure he will remember the exact distance between each number as well as the feelings in his sensitive fingers as he moves from one number to another."

When to Use

When the teacher believes the student needs to practice more care-fully in order to improve his intonation.

Inner Game

This mini-game is easy for most students to identify with, since almost everyone has marveled at the blind person's ability to function in a world designed for the seeing. It has the further advantage of suggesting great sensitivity in the student's touch.

Team Tactics

The Blind Man's Touch is for all string students.

Target Practice
Mini-Game 123

Outer Game

The teacher guides the student in finding a particular note in thumb position on the A string.

"Check to be sure that in this position your thumb is lying on its side across both the A and the D strings and that on the D string it sounds an octave below the third finger on the A string. Also, check to be sure there is a nice arch in your hand. Your base knuckles should point up and out. . . .

"Think about how your arm, hand, and fingers feel in this position and spacing. Look at the place on the fingerboard. Remember it. . . . Now, retaining this hand shape, lift your hand up in the air. You may even want to touch your head. Now return to the same place on the fingerboard. Let's hear it."

The target practice continues until the students become accurate at returning to the same pitch.

When to Use

After the student has a good start in thumb position.

Inner Game

Developing a memory for the location of notes on the fingerboard is essential to string playing. This mini-game is designed to make the student aware of the kinesthetic sense which makes it possible for a string player to remember the exact spot for each note.

Team Tactics

This mini-game as stated is for cello. However, target practice of any kind and the stressing of the kinesthetic sense are excellent for all string players.

The Exer-Cycle
Mini-Game 124

Outer Game

Teacher: "Today we're going to see how fast your fingers can run! First, place your left hand in a good position on the A string. Check your thumb to be sure that it gently touches the cello neck opposite your second finger. Next, with your base knuckles, flip your four fingers off the string and let them bounce back so their tips rest on an imaginary space platform. Raise your elbow slightly higher than usual.

"Now pretend you are a virtuoso! Move your fingers very fast in the air—just like lightning! Keep your fingers pointing down to the fingerboard even though they will not touch it. . . .

"Good! Go faster! Faster yet! Doesn't this remind you of those stationary bicycles in gyms that are used for exercising? The balance remains in the center of your hand just as it stays in the center of your body when you pedal. Supercurve your fingers!

"Now let the tips of your fingers drop to the string, but keep that same feeling. Your elbow will feel light, almost like a cloud floating in the sky, and your fingers will continue to move from their base knuckles."

The teacher leads the students into some fast repetitious finger exercises, slurring eight notes to a bow. Of course, each exercise will be practiced slowly at first, in order to establish the correct finger pattern and accurate intonation, but always with the same technique described above. Each should be repeated many times without pause. For example:

```
1 2 1 2 4 2 4 2
1 3 1 3 4 3 4 3
4 3 2 1 4 3 2 1
1 2 3 4 1 2 3 4
1 4 2 4 3 4 2 4
```

When to Use

At the teacher's discretion, after bowing and left hand technique are fairly well established. It can be used earlier if only the silent portion of the outer game is played, either in the air or on the upper bout of the cello.

Inner Game

The teacher recognizes the value of isolating certain techniques and performing them silently, either away from the cello or without touching the fingerboard. Once the general feeling of the action is discovered by the student and is fairly well established, she is usually able to transfer it to the cello with greater ease than if she had initially tried it on the instrument.

Also, the teacher is aware that fast technique on the cello is vastly different from slow technique, just as a person runs in an entirely different manner than he walks. Therefore, it is important that these differences be recognized and that passages which will be performed rapidly be first practiced slowly, using the actions required in the fast technique.

Should the student's fourth finger seem weak when she attempts these exercises, often a slight shifting of the balance point toward the fourth-finger side of the hand will help. However, care must be taken that once the optimum balance is obtained it remains in one place. The hand should not roll.

The reader may wish to refer to Mini-Game 91, *The Committee and Its Chairperson*, and Mini-Game 115, *The Space Platform*.

Team Tactics

This mini-game can be adapted to all stringed instruments.

The Sliding Thumb
Mini-Game 125

Outer Game

The teacher will conduct a review of Mini-Game 116, *Stretching the Elastic Index Finger*, and the playing of the first three notes of "Three Blind Mice." A mental photo will be taken of this extended position.

Teacher: "Today we'll learn how to play these notes in reverse. They will sound like the first three notes of a major scale or like the song 'Frère Jacques.' Here are the steps:

"1. Place your first finger on B on the A string. Your thumb will be under the note C, as usual.

"2. Now, while continuing to hold the pad of your first finger down on the same spot, let the base knuckle of your first finger sink in, moving closer to the cello neck. At the same time, your thumb will slide down the underside of the cello neck until it is opposite C♯. Your hand and forearm will glide forward with it. Watch your imaginary wristwatch while this motion occurs and turn your arm very slightly as though you plan to check the time.

"3. The instant your thumb reaches its destination, drop your second finger on C♯ and release the weight on the first. It's almost like your thumb had said to your second finger: 'I'll meet you at C♯.'

"4. Now, drop your fourth finger on D♯. He is such a naïve guy. He will feel exactly like he always does, because he hasn't had to stretch at all. It's as though he knew nothing had happened except that he went on a trip with your second and third fingers. He doesn't even know that the first fingertip was left behind, still hovering over B, and that it has changed its shape drastically since step 1.

"5. Look at your whole hand and forearm. Take a photo. Click! This photo should look exactly like the photo you took a few minutes ago."

When to Use

1. When introducing forward extensions of the left hand. This mini-game should always be preceded by Mini-Game 116, *Stretching the Elastic Index Finger*.
2. Anytime the teacher perceives that the student is stretching forward with her second, third, and/or fourth fingers, rather than stretching backward with her first finger.

Inner Game

The teacher knows that explaining the difference between forward

and backward extensions of the left hand is difficult, especially since they look exactly alike! In both cases the goal is to have the first finger be the only finger involved with stretching. Actually, the traditional terminology of forward and backward extensions is not a good description, since the fingers should never stretch forward toward the bridge.

The first phrase of "Au Claire de la Lune" may be used as an effective substitute for "Frère Jacques" in this mini-game. Great benefit is derived from playing either of these in all keys on each string in the first four positions. In fifth position and higher, the third finger should be used in place of the fourth.

The reader may wish to refer to Mini-Game 165, *Snapping the Rubber Band*, at this time.

Team Tactics

All noncellists may take a breather.

The Two-Hundred-Pound Man
Mini-Game 126

Outer Game

Teacher: "Let's all stand up. Imagine that we each weigh two hundred pounds! How many pounds are flowing through each foot?

"Yes, Helen, there are one hundred. Now shift all your weight so it flows through your left foot only. You can even lift your right foot off the floor.

"Next, shift your weight so all two hundred pounds are balanced on your right foot. Notice how flexible and springy the joints in your leg and foot feel despite all that weight going through them to the floor!

"This is the same way the weight is channeled through your playing finger only when you play slow passages. Let's try it now with your cello."

When to Use

Anytime the teacher perceives that the student is dividing the weight among her playing and supporting fingers or playing with stiff, tense fingers.

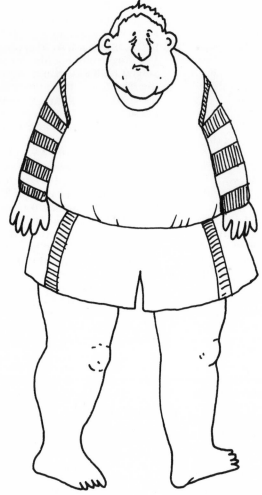

Mini-Game 126, *The Two-Hundred-Pound Man*

Inner Game

This mini-game is another method of demonstrating to the student that the energy flowing through her arm can be channeled through one finger and that that finger should still feel flexible. Care must be taken that the student does not roll or twist her hand when transferring the balance from one finger to another, because this is detrimental to accuracy in intonation and shifting.

Since this mini-game is not applicable to the playing of very fast passages, the reader may wish to see Mini-Game 124, *The Exer-Cycle*, at this time.

Team Tactics

Though *The Two-Hundred-Pound Man* is primarily intended for cello students, some of its ideas concerning the shifting of balance might be useful in teaching a violin or viola student with unusually small hands.

A Little Dog on a Leash
Mini-Game 127

Outer Game

Teacher: "When you practice this fast ascending scale passage up the fingerboard, think of a little dog on a long leash. Your hand is the little running dog and your arm is the long leash."

When to Use

When the student is playing a fast scale passage, either ascending or descending, which involves many shifts in position.

Mini-Game 127, *A Little Dog on a Leash*

Inner Game

The teacher recognizes the importance of the arm moving gracefully and continually in fast running passages, and not in jerks, as the hand moves from one position to another. This mini-game instantly conveys the mental image of the light, freely flowing leash, the role assumed by the arm.

Team Tactics

This mini-game is applicable to all stringed instruments.

APPROACHES TO ESTABLISHING THE LEFT HAND POSITION BY COMBINING MINI-GAMES

Five approaches using combinations of mini-games to help establish a good, workable cello left hand position are presented on the following pages. They are described primarily as examples of the many available possibilities. Others limited only by the imagination of the teacher can be created by him.

Before using any of the following approaches, it is recommended that the fingerboard of the student's cello be marked with adhesive-backed tapes or dots in at least two places: first, a major second above the open strings; second, a perfect fourth above the open strings. Since the student undoubtedly will have already experienced placing her hand in first position according to her method book, and since these approaches will most likely serve as alternatives, not every detail of the hand position is described in any single approach.

The experienced teacher recommends the advisability of shaping the entire hand by using all four

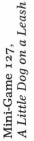

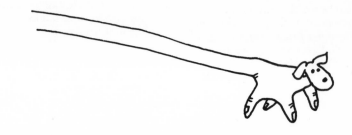

fingers in the initial introduction to left hand technique, even though the first music presented in the method book may require only one or two fingers. This can easily be done by placing the entire hand in position, then lifting those fingers not immediately needed, thereby insuring that the student's hand and arm alignment will not have to be changed when new notes are added.

When the position needs correcting, it is generally better to have the student remove his hand completely and make a fresh start rather than attempt to adjust within the existing faulty position. Also, as a rule, it is preferable to use one of the inner strings when introducing any new technique and, then, immediately transfer this new position to the other strings.

The Free Ride Approach

Outer Game

Teacher: "Place three fingers on the D string any place on the fingerboard near the bridge. Arch your hand and fingers nicely like a rainbow. Now, with your arm doing all the work, pull your hand back to first position. It's as though the string is getting wiped and your hand is having a free ride!

"When you reach first position, add your fourth finger and slip your thumb under the neck opposite your second finger. Then bob your left elbow up and down and around to find the spot which makes your finger pads cling to the fingerboard best.

"Check to be sure that your hand forms a tunnel large enough for a butterfly to fly through and that you can jiggle your shoulders like a dancing puppet. Let's hear you play. Remember the weight channels through the playing finger only."

When to Use

1. After the posture and placement of the cello have been established.
2. Anytime the teacher thinks a review or an alternative approach is in order.
3. Whenever the teacher believes that the present position of the student's left hand and arm may not allow graceful shifting

to and from the higher positions on the fingerboard.

Inner Game

Since much of cello playing involves shifting up and down the fingerboard, *The Free Ride Approach* insures that the position of the left hand and arm will be ready for this type of activity. The chances for a tight wrist or thumb are alleviated.

The reader may wish to refer to the following mini-games used in this approach:
98, *The Arch of a Rainbow*
90, *The Buoy*
87, *The Butterfly Tunnel*
18, *The Puppet Dance*

The Indian War Dance Approach

Outer Game

Teacher: "Have you heard an Indian war dance? Remember its haunting rhythm? BOOM-boom-boom-boom, BOOM-boom-boom-boom . . . Monkey see, monkey do."

The teacher taps the upper bout of her cello or a desk with her left hand in this accented rhythm. Her fingers are arched and spaced somewhat apart; her finger pads form a straight line. As she taps, her whole arm jiggles. The students imitate her.

"Now we're going to do this on the fingerboard. Place your hand gently on the D string with your first and fourth finger pads on the tapes. Your fingers will be curved and evenly spaced. Your thumb will go under the cello neck opposite your second finger. It will barely touch the neck and will be straight. When I face you, I should not be able to see your thumb. Hide it from me! Your first finger will tilt slightly back toward the cello tuning pegs.

"As you hold your thumb in place, lift your hand high so all four fingers point down to the string. Their pads will form a magic dotted line—dot, dot, dot—which is almost parallel to the string and about an inch or so above it. It's as though they are resting on an imaginary string which is directly above the real string. The base knuckles of your fingers form another magic dotted

line—dot, dot, dot—which is also almost parallel to the string.

"Now drop your fingers, as one unit, on the string in a tapping fashion so you can hear an Indian war dance. BOOM-boom-boom-boom."

The teacher will take care that the students do not turn their shoulders in order to look at their hands.

"It is important for a cellist to learn to look out of the corner of his eye so he doesn't twist his shoulders. Check yourself by shrugging. Also, check your elbow placement by bobbing it into a spot that makes the Indian war dance sound the loudest."

After the students perform this successfully, the teacher leads them into playing. She demonstrates on the student's arm how the weight should flow only through the finger that is actually producing the pitch. She gradually leads the students to the playing of a simple tune, such as "Hot Cross Buns," on all strings.

When to Use

1. At an early lesson after the posture and placement of the cello have been established.
2. Whenever the teacher believes a review or an alternative approach is in order.
3. Anytime the student's left hand is held too low to allow the lifting and dropping of his fingers from the base knuckles.

Inner Game

The teacher knows that tapping out the Indian war dance almost inevitably forces the student's arm, hand, and fingers into a desirable position. Although the lifting and dropping action of the fingers from their base knuckles is stressed, it is almost impossible to tap out this accented rhythm without an arm alignment which allows both strength and flexibility.

The teacher is also aware of the importance of the student's shrugging his shoulders periodically when giving special attention to his left hand, particularly in first position. Since it is a strain to raise and lower his shoulders while in a twisted position, this action will force the student to sit in a good playing posture.

The reader may wish to refer to the inner games of the following mini-games:

The Broom Handle Approach

Outer Game

Teacher: "Monkey see, monkey do! Wrap your left hand around your cello neck so your fourth finger covers the second tape. Hold the neck in the same sticky, clinging manner as you hold a broom handle when you sweep. Let your arm hang. Since there is a feeling of suction between your hand and the wood, nothing is tense.

"Now slowly pull your hand across the fingerboard until your fingers are on the D string in a playing position. You'll feel almost like you are dragging your fingers across rubber. Let your hand and wrist rise slightly as your finger pads reach their destination. Note how your first finger slants slightly toward the scroll.

"Next, check your thumb to be sure it is under the cello neck opposite your second finger. It should be straight but not pushing up. Allow all the weight of your arm to channel through your playing finger, which in this case is the fourth finger.

"Now bob your left elbow up and down like a buoy in water. Discover where it creates the feeling of the most suction between your fourth finger pad and the fingerboard. This will show you the best elbow level for playing on this string. Let's hear this note."

Next the teacher will guide the student in repeating the process, this time landing on the third finger, then the second, and finally the first.

"Remember that the weight will flow through your playing finger only, although your supporting fingers will sit on the string like zombies."

When to Use

1. Anytime a review or an alternative approach is desired.

2. Whenever the teacher observes that the student does not appear to have enough suction in her finger pads or does not have her left arm aligned with her fourth finger.

Inner Game

This approach emphasizes the feeling of suction. It is especially helpful because the hand starts from a point near the centerline of the player's body.

The reader may wish to refer to the following mini-games:

The Rapping Approach

Outer Game

Teacher: "Make a gentle fist with your left hand. Now rap on the fingerboard all the way up toward the bridge and back. It's as though you are rapping on a door.

"When your fist returns to first position, open it up without disturbing your arm alignment and allow your finger pads to sink into the D string. Slip your thumb gently under the cello neck opposite your second finger.

"The profile of your left hand will look like four mountain peaks. There will be a direct route between your elbow and your base knuckles, like a freeway with no hills, valleys, winding curves, or detours. Your thumb will feel like elastic. Channel all the weight through the finger that determines the pitch. Let's hear you play."

When to Use

1. Anytime a review or an alternative approach is needed.
2. Whenever the teacher notices that the student's hand is not aligned well with her arm or is so low that it shows very little profile, thus restricting its maneuverability.

Inner Game

Knocking on the fingerboard insures that the energy is channeled

through from the trunk of the body, although the student concentrates on the hand itself. Thus, the teacher can be reasonably well assured that the alignment of the hand, wrist, and arm is correct and that no tension is present in the upper arm.

The reader may wish to refer to the following mini-games used in this approach:

The Great Fall Approach

Outer Game

Teacher: "Look at the side of your left index finger. Now shape your hand as though you are holding something nice and round, such as an orange or a peach. Since the fruit is rather large, your fingers will be curved and spread somewhat apart. In fact, there should be room to insert an extra finger between each of your fingers. Test this with your right hand. . . . Let the fruit vanish but maintain your hand position.

"Next, push your right index finger against all four tips of your left hand fingers so they form a straight line. Or, if you prefer, line them up on your bow stick. Notice how your second and third fingers had to arch a little bit more in order to form this line. Let your first finger tilt back slightly toward your thumb. Remove your right hand or bow stick.

"While retaining this form, place your hand on top of your head so only the finger pads touch your hair. Relax your arm so all its weight flows through your four finger pads. Don't let any other part of your hand touch your head. Doesn't it feel like your finger pads are sinking right down into your scalp? Notice how flexible and spongy your fingers are as you jiggle them slightly. It feels almost like you're massaging your scalp. Your finger pads seem to sink in deeper and deeper!

"Keeping your hand, fingers, and arm in this same form and allowing them to move as one unit, lift your hand off your head. Then, pull down with your elbow and upper arm so your finger pads land heavily on the fingerboard. It's as though they are sinking into a soft rubber fingerboard after a great fall."

After the students have completed several successful falls, the teacher adds:

"This time we'll do it a little differently. Place your hand in the same position on your scalp, but shift the weight of your arm and hand slightly so all the energy seems to flow through your fourth finger pad only. Your other finger pads will just sit there like zombies. Now fall to the D string, allowing all the energy to flow through your fourth finger to the second tape. Good! Play this note with your bow so we can hear how nice it sounds."

After the students have repeated this several times, the teacher adds:

"Slip your thumb gently under the cello neck opposite your second finger pad. It goes almost straight out and should not push up. The feeling in your hand and arm does not change in any way."

The teacher will gradually lead the students into falling on three fingers with the weight only on the third finger, then two, etc. The fall will be made to various selected spots on the fingerboard, including all strings and all positions, and the energy will always be focused through the finger determining the pitch.

When to Use

1. Anytime a review or an alternative approach is needed.
2. Whenever the teacher senses that not enough natural weight is flowing through the student's fingers and that he is using a grabbing or a pushing action.
3. Whenever the student shows a tendency to push up with his thumb.

Inner Game

An advantage of this approach from the head is that a good alignment of the left hand and arm is almost guaranteed. Since there is no mention of the thumb until after the sensation of falling into the fingerboard is discovered, all emphasis is on the downward pressure brought about by the weight of the arm. Thus, any tendency to squeeze the cello neck will be alleviated.

An added benefit is that the student will feel no need to push the string down by exerting extra pressure with his fingers, because the fall was initiated by the downward pull of his arm. Later the same feeling can be acquired without the great fall.

The reader may wish to refer to the following mini-games:

CHECKPOINTS FOR HOME PRACTICE

Three lists of checkpoints for the cello student are given as examples of the ways mini-games may be used for his home practice. Similar lists may be devised for the other stringed instruments.

List I

1. Are your fingers spaced evenly with the first and fourth finger pads on the tapes? Is there room for an imaginary finger between each so you could have an eight-fingered hand?
2. Is there a magic dotted line running straight from your left elbow through the base knuckle of your second finger, curving to the nice soft finger pad?
3. Is it easy for you to slide your finger pads up and down the fingerboard like you are wiping the string?
4. Do your left hand fingers have a nice profile? Do your fingers look like four birds sitting on a fence, with the second being the tallest and the third the next tallest?
5. Does your first finger lean slightly so its second knuckle is closer to the scroll than its fingernail?
6. Is your thumb straight? Does it feel like elastic?
7. Can you easily flap your left elbow like a rooster getting ready to crow "Cock-a-doodle-doo!" while your hand clings to the fingerboard?
8. Do your hand and the cello neck form a tunnel so you can see light through it?
9. Is the energy from your arm flowing through the playing finger only? Do your other fingers feel like cooked macaroni although they retain their shape?
10. Are your shoulders still even? Not a bit twisted? Can you bob them up and down like a dancing puppet?

The reader may wish to refer to the following mini-games:

List II

1. Can you easily rap on the fingerboard all the way up toward the bridge and back?
2. Is your hand arched over the fingerboard like a rainbow when playing on the lower strings?
3. Does your elbow feel like it is floating?
4. Is the freeway between your elbow and your base knuckles straight? Is it free of hills, valleys, winding curves, and detours?
5. When your fingers spring up, do they point down toward the string like four divers aiming for the water?
6. If your fingerboard were alive, would it be aware of only your playing finger?
7. Are you treating the neck of your cello tenderly?
8. Does your left hand profile show four mountain peaks, with the second being the tallest?
9. Is the magic line formed by your base knuckles almost parallel to the string or the edge of the fingerboard?
10. Can you easily shrug your shoulders?

The reader may wish to refer to the following mini-games:

List III

1. Does your hand feel like it is shaped around a rather large fruit, such as an orange or a peach?
2. Is the tunnel formed by your hand and the cello neck large enough for a butterfly to fly through?
3. Is the power line between your elbow and your base knuckles free of all kinks, like a good water hose? (See Mini-Game 144, *The Good Water Hose*, in the following chapter.)
4. Is all the weight of your arm channeled through the playing finger? Is your playing finger definitely the chairperson of the committee?
5. How fast can you move your left hand from the nut to the bridge and back without touching the strings?
6. Does your thumb feel soft and elastic as it touches the neck of your cello? Is it straight?
7. Can you tap out an Indian war dance rhythm convincingly? Does this action make your upper arm have a slight rolling motion?
8. Is your playing finger sinking into the fingerboard as though it is made of rubber?
9. Would your elbow make a good buoy floating in the water?
10. Can you easily rock sideways with your cello?

The reader may wish to refer to the following mini-games:

9 Mini-Games for Varied Purposes

Just as the football coach holds in reserve trick plays for certain purposes, the pro in the game of string teaching saves special moves for specific situations.

The twenty-four mini-games in this chapter may be used when the teacher believes the time is right. All are designed to help the student realize his potential. Particular emphasis is placed on home practice, which, after all, is the final determinant of the success of the total game.

Handle with Care
Mini-Game 128

Outer Game

Teacher: "Since we want our cellos to sing and sound alive, it's a good idea to treat them like people. Take care not to bump or scratch them, and it's important not to expose them to extreme temperatures. Be careful about leaving them in a car. If it's too cold or too hot for you to feel comfortable sitting in a closed-up, parked car for a period of time, it's also too cold or too hot for your cello.

"I'll give you more details about taking care of your cello at your next lesson. Meanwhile, treat it with kindness!"

When to Use

At a young student's first lesson.

Inner Game

The first lesson is much too short to accomplish all that needs to be done. Not only must the teacher make certain that the instrument will not be harmed before the next lesson, but she also recognizes the psychological importance for the student to learn how to hold his cello and to produce some kind of sound. Above all, she knows that the youngster must leave his lesson with a feeling of excitement and accomplishment and an eagerness to return.

The analogy given in this mini-game helps the teacher convey an important general concept in a very few seconds. When possible, it is recommended that a lecture-demonstration concerning the care of instruments be given to parents of new students at an orientation session preceding the first lesson.

Team Tactics

All musical instruments should be handled with care.

Footprints in the Snow
Mini-Game 129

Outer Game

Teacher: "Picture in your mind's eye some freshly fallen snow several inches deep. There is not a mark on it except for a series of ten footprints made by one person. They form an interesting pattern—some steps are very close together, others are far apart! Obviously, for three or four steps, the person must have tiptoed. At one time he must have leaped!

"Now I challenge you with this mental game. You are to follow this person's path exactly, matching your footprints to his so that not one extra mark is made in that beautiful snow. I'll give you a minute or two to practice this six times. Then, before the seventh time you walk this path you'll be blindfolded. Think carefully when you practice. Go slowly and measure each step. And, most important of all, *remember* how you did it.

"This is exactly what we do when we practice music. Approach each step carefully—think and remember!"

When to Use

Anytime the teacher feels that the student would benefit from this explanation of how to practice.

Inner Game

The teacher is aware that much practice time is wasted because the student is not conscious of the mental processes involved. Too often she will use a trial-and-error method, constantly making and repeating mistakes. Undoing a mistake and having to change an ingrained muscular pattern take more time than learning to play something correctly in the first place. Also, in the case of bad intonation, there is danger that the student's ear will adapt to the faulty pitch, thereby making correction doubly difficult.

Team Tactics

This mini-game is designed for all string students.

Speedier than CB
Mini-Game 130

Outer Game

Teacher: "One of the most amazing things about our bodies is the terrific communication line between our brains and our hands. For example, when a musician sees the notes B, C♯, D on a page of music in a fast tempo, her fingers and bow arm will have already played them before she could possibly have said, 'Play 1, 3, 4 on the A string!' It is speedier than CB!

"We can save much time in our class by training our hands to respond just as quickly when we hear instructions. Let's see how quickly you can get the message through to your hands when I call out some commands.

"Right hand, touch these places: your nose, your left ear, your fingerboard, your C string, your scroll, your bridge. Left hand, touch these places: your head, your right shoulder, your chin, your A string, your tailpiece, your D string tuning peg. Now, touch your nose with your right hand, point to your bridge with your left hand. . . ."

When to Use

1. Early in the training.
2. Anytime the teacher wishes to speed up responses.

Inner Game

The teacher realizes that most students are capable of responding very fast but can be quite sluggish unless challenged. With frequent drills of this kind, the students' reactions will become more rapid and they will benefit enormously. The chances of sending a message to the wrong hand and then having to make a correction will be greatly reduced with just a little concentrated effort.

Team Tactics

All good buddies of the string class can play this mini-game.

Turning up the Volume
Mini-Game 131

Outer Game

Teacher: "I believe I'll turn up the volume."

As though he is walking up to an FM radio, the teacher takes a step or two forward and makes a dramatic gesture of turning the imaginary knob which controls the volume.

When to Use

Whenever the students are playing too softly.

Inner Game

Most beginning and intermediate cello students need repeated encouragement to play louder. Because of their fear of making the proverbial scratchy, ugly sounds associated with stringed instruments played by beginners, many take refuge in playing softly by drawing the bow close to the fingerboard with very little pressure. This can be quite harmful if it becomes a habit.

The teacher knows that one necessary ingredient for producing a good tone on the cello is live weight flowing from the player's body through her arm and hand to the top of her bow stick; this, in turn, causes the bow hair to sink into the string. When less volume is desired, the player should suspend some of the weight of her arm. The teacher believes that students who are permitted to play softly most of the time have no infallible means of being sure that their arm and hand alignment and the relationship between the hand and bow are correct. He considers that the very act of playing loudly without a harsh quality is one of the best possible means of checking this.

Should the student be unable to play with a big full tone, it is a sure indication that something is wrong and that the flow of energy is probably restricted or misdirected. Furthermore, the cello student who habitually suspends her arm weight will find it very difficult to let go and will undoubtedly compensate by pushing down with her fingers when asked to play loudly. This action must be avoided because of the resulting hard sound. In the long run, the teacher who repeatedly turns up the volume when a student plays shyly does her a great service.

The reader is advised to see Mini-Game 60, *The Recipe for a Big Tone*.

Team Tactics

The outer game of *Turning up the Volume* is good for all string students.

The Instant Replay
Mini-Game 132

Outer Game

Teacher: "Let's see and hear an instant replay of that measure. Run it by again slowly!"

The teacher shows the student how to use this device in home practice for detecting and remedying problems or weaknesses.

When to Use

Anytime in the training to help the student learn practice techniques.

Inner Game

The teacher is aware that students continually need to be shown how to practice. She seeks every opportunity to inject fresh ideas, or even just new ways of saying the same thing, in order to keep home practice methods from growing stale.

Team Tactics

Instant replays in home practice are essential to all instrumentalists.

Mini-Game 133, Keep a Cool Head

Keep a Cool Head
Mini-Game 133

Outer Game

Teacher: "Some of us have to be careful that our heads don't get so carried away that they begin to dance when we make music! Cello playing can become unnecessarily difficult if your head starts beating out the rhythm or jerking on the downbeat. I want to show you why. Put your cellos aside while we play some golf."

The teacher leads the students into some imaginary golf strokes until their forms are mutually admired.

"Now try bobbing or jerking your head while you hit another hole in one."

After the students discover for themselves the disturbing effect of such actions, the teacher will add: "If your head moves from time to time, it should move gently and should never appear to be a separate part of your body. Your beat is internal; no single part of your anatomy should serve as a metronome. Be smart! Keep a cool head!"

When to Use

When the student bobs, jerks, or shakes his head while playing.

Inner Game

The teacher recognizes that this undesirable characteristic is actually an indication that the student is totally involved and probably has an unusually intense musical feeling. In fact, he will probably be surprised to learn that his head has been dancing. Though this can be interpreted as a positive sign, the teacher has the responsibility of guarding against any habit that could be detrimental to the student's progress.

Team Tactics

All string players need cool heads.

The Super Sleuth
Mini-Game 134

Outer Game

Teacher: "Be a super sleuth in your home practice! Use your magnifying glass to hunt for clues to the note or group of notes that could possibly be weak in a public performance. Strengthen them with careful, slow practice; then blend them back into the context of the music. In this way you will gain confidence. You'll know that you could finish your piece even if a group of little baby kangaroos should come hopping into the room."

When to Use

Anytime in the training to help the student learn how to practice.

Inner Game

The teacher knows that confidence building is self-perpetuating. The student who gives a successful public performance will look forward to the next one with more confidence. The pupil who was embarrassed because she felt she played poorly will dread the next. Therefore, the teacher looks on any kind of public performance at every level of advancement with seriousness. Naturally the basis for confidence building is for the student to know the music so well that she can play it under any conditions.

The sleuth's magnifying glass can also be a great help by exaggerating problems in home practice. For example, if a crossing between two adjacent strings gives trouble with either hand, exaggerating the same motions by crossing to the next farther string can make the trouble spot seem easier. That is, if a crossing from the A string to the D string poses a problem, the act of going from the A string to the G or C string a few times can ease the A to D crossing. This is similar to the long-distance runner's wearing of weights on his ankles before an important race. When the weights are removed, his feet will feel much lighter.

Team Tactics

All fine musicians are exceptional sleuths in home practice!

The Virtuoso
Mini-Game 135

Outer Game

Teacher: "Set aside your cellos and bows. We won't need them for this mini-game. . . . Let's pretend that you are a fantastic cello virtuoso! Pantomime playing a fast piece that goes all over an imaginary fingerboard. Don't forget your imaginary bow. Play brilliantly!"

When to Use

Anytime except in the earliest training.

Inner Game

The teacher knows that a natural feeling for cello playing can be acquired through such an activity. Since the student knows that she can do no wrong, all fears and tensions are eliminated. Meanwhile, the teacher watches the positions and motions used in the pantomiming and compares them with those demonstrated by the same student in an actual performance only moments later. Quickly he will discover the differences and point them out to the student, so the necessary adjustments can be made.

Team Tactics

Pantomimed virtuosic technique can give any string student a boost.

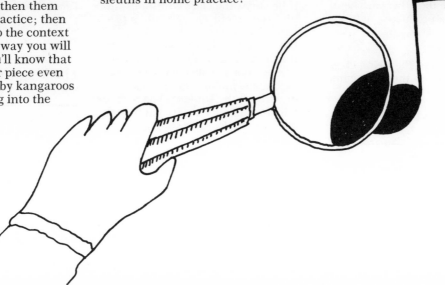

Turn off the Sound
Mini-Game 136

Outer Game

Teacher: "I'd like for you to play this piece again, but this time turn off the sound."

The students pretend that they are performing on television but that the sound has been turned off. While the teacher plays either his cello or the piano, the students pantomime a performance.

This can be done in several ways but is usually most beneficial under these conditions: (1) when the left hand actions are executed in the air with only the thumb contacting the cello in its usual place under the neck; the hand will be above the appropriate string with the fingers pointing down to the fingerboard; and (2) when the bowing is mimed without the bow itself.

When to Use

1. To free the students of the responsibility of producing tones so they can concentrate on the notes and the motions required.
2. To eliminate the students' sound so the teacher will be able to spot possible problems and misunderstandings faster.
3. To hear an individual student play.
4. When a student is holding her left hand and wrist too low.

Inner Game

This mini-game is especially effective in class teaching, since it allows each student to perform by herself while the others are kept occupied in a productive activity.

Team Tactics

Every member of the string class can participate in this mini-game.

Bridge Builders
Mini-Game 137

Outer Game

Teacher: "When a fine musician practices, she listens carefully for notes that need special attention, then focuses in on them. After she can play them well, she practices linking them to the surrounding music by starting a few notes earlier and going a little farther. I think of her as being a good bridge builder!

"When we hear students perform, it's easy to discern whether or not they have built bridges in their home practice. The music of those who have flows from one note to the next, much like the words of a fluent speaker. The performance of students who don't build bridges is made up of hesitations and sometimes even stops and starts. We don't want that! Let's go through your piece now and practice building bridges."

When to Use

1. Early in the training when teaching a student how to practice.
2. Anytime a student's performance has halts or hesitations.

Inner Game

One of the most disheartening and sometimes exasperating experiences a teacher can have is working with a student who habitually stops and starts. At times getting a person to play even four measures without interruption can become a monumental victory! While this usually indicates a lack of practice, sometimes it is simply a matter of habit. At other times it can stem from a lack of confidence.

When a student is a member of a class, there is much less chance of his adopting this undesirable characteristic; he soon learns that, if he stops, the class continues the phrase without him. Should a private student have this tendency, the teacher's playing with him on the piano or a stringed instrument can be enormously beneficial, providing she finishes the phrase with or without the student. The teacher who forbids this deadly habit from creeping in does her student a great service.

Team Tactics

This mini-game is for all music students.

Sound Effects
Mini-Game 138

Outer Game

Teacher: "Let's take a break from your assigned music and make some sound effects with your instruments."

He continues by asking if any member of the class has discovered a sound effect she would like to demonstrate and teach her fellow students.

When to Use

Whenever the teacher feels the class would benefit from such a change in concentration.

Inner Game

Every teacher, no matter how fine, has experienced days when he cannot get the class off the ground. Even though he tries to arouse enthusiasm, for some reason or other the class seems lifeless.

If this mini-game is reserved for such an occasion, it can both enliven the class spirit and provide a learning experience. Anytime a string player discovers how to make a sound effect, either pleasant or unpleasant, she is getting better acquainted with her instrument. Furthermore, while teaching others how to produce a specific sound, she also learns how to avoid it. Obviously, this mini-game should not be overused and should be immediately followed by an emphasis on the creation of beautiful tones, making a dramatic contrast to some of the sound effects.

Team Tactics

Every music student enjoys and benefits from *Sound Effects*.

The Magic Centerline
Mini-Game 139

Outer Game

Teacher: "I like to watch the centerline of a fine cellist because to me it's part of the magic of nature. I can imagine an invisible dotted line running from the floor up through his back to the top of his head.

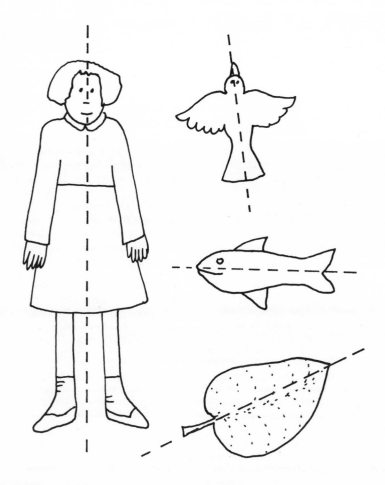

Mini-Game 139, *The Magic Centerline*

"Look around you and you will always find a vital centerline. Watch a bird fly! Note how its wings balance and work perfectly from the centerline. Observe the fish swim! Both the wings of a bird and the fins of a fish are powerless unless they are connected to their centerlines. Notice how the sweetest and most gentle dog will snarl if he considers his back is in danger!

"Now let's picture a beautiful tree. In your imagination, strip it of its leaves and watch the life-giving sap flow through the roots hidden underground, up through its trunk, and out through its branches. Study a leaf under a magnifying glass and witness the network of veins which derive their source from the trunk, via the branches and twigs.

"As a cellist, prize your centerline. Try to keep your body balanced—just as nature intended—so the energy flows from it through 'our arms to your hands."

When to Use

Whenever the teacher thinks it appropriate, but probably not too early in the training.

Inner Game

This mini-game speaks for itself. The teacher constantly observes nature and derives inspiration and knowledge from it with the hope of helping her students.

Team Tactics

The balance stressed in this outer game is important to all string players.

Speed Thinking
Mini-Game 140

Outer Game

Teacher: "Today let's pretend you are members of the Chicago Symphony and I am the conductor. Since all pros are very fast think-ers and can follow directions in-stantly, let's practice this now. I'll announce where we will start in the music, then give you only a split second to find the place and be ready to go. Let's see if you can be with me on the first beat I con-duct!"

The teacher proceeds by calling out directions. In each case only a measure or two will be played be-fore he quickly announces the next instruction.

"Start at the top of page 5. . . . Start before letter D, three meas-ures. . . . Start on the F♯ in the fifth measure. . . ."

When to Use

Anytime after the students can read notes.

Inner Game

The teacher's goal is to motivate his students to take pride in being fast thinkers. Since most young people are capable of thinking and moving fast, the secret lies in chal-lenging the students to meet their teacher's expectations, to win their peers' admiration, and to take per-sonal pride in being speedy.

An added benefit is that many discipline problems will be solved when the pace of the class quick-ens and there is less opportunity for minds to wander. Soon the stu-dent who has habitually asked the teacher to repeat directions will lis-ten more attentively and appear more alert.

Team Tactics

Speed Thinking is for all instru-mental music students.

Finger Memory
Mini-Game 141

Outer Game

Teacher: "The wise cellist thinks and consciously memorizes when she practices. But, after she has played a phrase carefully many times, she will discover that her fingers and arms also have a mem-ory! In preparation for your next lesson, practice this technical pas-sage so well that you can play it over and over without thinking

Mini-Game 141, *Finger Memory*

Hamburgers and Mints
Mini-Game 142

Outer Game

Teacher: "Today I brought some imaginary refreshments. Help yourself to a nice thick hamburger. Isn't it delicious? Now let's top it off with a mint.

"Freeze! Notice how your mouth is preparing for the little thin mint compared to the big thick hamburger a moment ago! This is the way we instinctively prepare our mouths for anything we eat; the same is true of our hands.

"Your hands should always forecast the type of passage they are getting ready to play. Your left hand, for example, will feel different when the approaching phrase is fast and light, calling for dancing fingers on the A string, than when it is a dark slow passage on the heavy C string. Even your bow hand prepares for the feel and mood of the forthcoming phrase."

When to Use

Whenever the teacher thinks it appropriate, but not too early in the training.

Inner Game

The teacher is relating a natural phenomenon to cello playing. If the student prepares himself mentally for the type of action required by the forthcoming passage, his chances of executing it successfully are greatly increased.

Team Tactics

Hamburgers and Mints provides nourishment for all string students.

while I tell you a story, never missing a note!"

A suggested story follows.

"Did you know that European cuckoos, the birds who sing a descending minor third, don't go in for homemaking and child rearing? Instead, they place their kids in foster homes! This is the way they go about it.

"The mother cuckoo watches birds of another species build a cozy, inviting nest. Then she waits until they are away from home, goes to the nest, tosses out one of their eggs, and replaces it with one of her own. Usually she visits twelve nests and leaves twelve eggs.

"Strangely enough, the foster parents never guess what has happened and raise the baby cuckoo as their own daughter or son. Can you imagine what a little sparrow is thinking when he drops seeds into the gaping mouth of a hungry baby bird twice his size? And what a surprise when the youngster begins singing his own special song!"

When to Use

Anytime after several months of study, when the teacher thinks the student is devoting insufficient time to practice.

Inner Game

The teacher recognizes that the remarkable ability of the human body to memorize the sensation of bodily positions and motions is what makes it possible to learn such an intricate skill as cello playing. The development of this kinesthetic sense comes through repetition, which is one of the principal reasons for home practice. However, it is only after the student learns to play a passage well at a slower tempo that it should be repeated innumerable times.

Conversely, it is this same phenomenal ability that makes the unlearning of bad habits so difficult. Thus, extreme caution must be taken so that only desirable motions are repeated.

The story of the fascinating cuckoo is used as an example of the teacher's being on the constant lookout for every opportunity to ignite the student's imagination and appreciation for all forms of life.

Team Tactics

This mini-game is for all instrumental students.

Mini-Game 142, *Hamburgers and Mints*

Mini-Game 143, The Magic Potion

USE AS DIRECTED

The Magic Potion
Mini-Game 143

Outer Game

When the teacher spots a persistent problem in a position or an action which has not been corrected by the student in her home practice, he says:

"I see that your fourth finger is still giving you trouble. We'll fix that! This morning I brewed up a magic invisible potion especially for this problem. Let's apply some of it to your fourth finger. . . . Now play your piece again. . . .

"Good! It works! Keep some of this handy when you practice and apply it mentally every few seconds until the problem is completely solved!"

When to Use
Anytime a bad habit persists because the student has not remembered to replace it with a good one in her home practice.

Inner Game

The teacher recognizes that a little added drama can make a lesson more effective, fun, and unforgettable. Furthermore, he recognizes that a good habit can replace a bad one only if the mind of the player constantly flashes a reminder to the physical part involved.

Team Tactics

Since music itself seems to have a magical quality, the handy potion described above can be a useful prop in any instrumental music class.

The Good Water Hose
Mini-Game 144

Outer Game

Teacher: "I like to think of a cellist's arms as being like two good water hoses running from his body to his bow and fingerboard. As you know, a hose is usually made of rubber or soft plastic and is extremely pliable. It can assume almost any shape. Yet it conducts a terrific power as the water flows through it.

"Anyone who has watered a garden knows that the secret lies in not allowing a kink to form in the hose, because it restricts the power line from the faucet. She is also aware that any kind of pressure, such as a person's foot or a brick, on any part of the hose can reduce the water flow to a trickle. Let's play now and check your water hoses to be sure that the energy flows through them freely."

When to Use

Whenever the teacher thinks it appropriate except in the very first lessons.

Inner Game

This mini-game explains in simple language the basis for the teacher's approach to cello playing and teaching. He considers it his role to free the body so the true spirit of the player is able to be communicated through the music. He constantly looks for any physical characteristic that could possibly prevent or restrict this natural flow.

Team Tactics

Most string students can benefit from this analogy.

Tackling a Problem
Mini-Game 145

Outer Game

Teacher: "When you have a problem in cello playing, there's only one way to go about solving it— meet it head on. It won't go away if you look in the other direction!

"Think of the doctor who looks at her desperately sick patient. She doesn't say: 'Mercy, he is sick all over. There's nothing that can be done—I don't know the cause of his illness.' Instead, she checks everything in search for the original source of the trouble, usually working through the process of elimination.

"We too can be good diagnosticians in our home practice. If you know something is wrong but don't know exactly what, isolate each technique. For example, check out the left hand by playing the passage pizzicato. No problem? OK, move to the bow. Play the bowing pattern on one open string, then on all the strings involved. Check each string crossing, etc. Soon you will pinpoint the problem, just as the doctor may find that an infect-

Mini-Game 145, Tackling a Problem

ed tooth was the source of a raging fever and a crippling pain in the joints.

"Be smart. Play the role of a cool, objective diagnostician at the appropriate times."

When to Use

Anytime the teacher thinks it appropriate, but not too early in the training.

Inner Game

The teacher knows that the isolation of problems is an enormous timesaver and can be used effectively by all students. It also makes string teaching and playing a fascinating experience when the teacher and student solve problems by tackling them aggressively.

In the special case of developing a beautiful vibrato, however, the advice of meeting a problem head on may not be appropriate. It is recommended that the reader refer to the section entitled "Tactics of the String Teacher When Introducing the Vibrato" in chapter 12.

Team Tactics

This mini-game can be used by all string students.

Undoing the Dog-Ear
Mini-Game 146

Outer Game

Teacher: "The wise cellist often exaggerates in her practice. For example, if her goal is to curve her fingers more, she will often practice supercurving them. I'll show you why.

"Let's take these papers which have had their corners dog-eared and straighten them so they lie flat like new paper. . . . Look what you're doing! You folded them just as far the other way in order to undo the dog-ears. Let's apply this principle to your cello practice."

When to Use

Whenever the teacher has given repeated advice, such as "Curve your fingers," without achieving the desired result.

Inner Game

Through experience the teacher knows that sometimes it appears that even the most conscientious and receptive student has not heard her advice. Often, for example, a student will think he is making a crescendo, yet none is audible; perhaps only a recording of his performance will convince him that this has not happened. By exaggerating an action even a few times, the student can save many hours of practice.

Team Tactics

All music students can play this mini-game.

What's My Mood?
Mini-Game 147

Outer Game

Teacher: "Today we're going to play *What's My Mood?*—an extended version of *Turn off the Sound*. We will take this one piece and show all the different moods it can express. The composer gave no title, tempo indication, or dynamic markings. Let's find all the various ways it can be played.

"Turn off the sound. The TV viewer should be able to recognize the mood of the piece even though he can't hear it!"

The students will pantomime playing the piece as a march, a prayer, a dance, etc.; only the teacher's performance at the piano will be heard. Later the sound will be turned on.

"Remember, if the sound is to be dramatic, your gestures must be dramatic. Energetic sounds are produced by energetic motions. Even your preparatory motions should anticipate the mood of the music."

When to Use

Anytime the teacher thinks it will help the students gain the concept that the characteristics of a tone or phrase will reflect the physical motions that generate it. It should not precede Mini-Game 136, *Turn off the Sound.*

Inner Game

The teacher knows that this mini-game is fun for a class and that it helps the students discover a very important basic principle. At another lesson it can be changed into a guessing game. Each student can pantomime a piece while the other students guess what mood is being portrayed.

Team Tactics

Every member of the string class can play *What's My Mood?*

Looking Ahead
Mini-Game 148

Outer Game

Teacher: "A person who sight-reads music well reminds me of an alert driver who keeps her eyes on the road and is aware of every vehicle, pedestrian, and street sign some distance ahead. She doesn't just drive up to a traffic signal, look at it, then slam on the brakes!

"Let's work at developing the habit of looking ahead in your music. The trick lies in playing one measure while your eyes scan the next measure or measures.

"Begin reading this piece. When I snap my fingers, close your eyes instantly and see how long you can continue playing! We'll count the number of notes you can play after I signal. Remember, the secret lies in looking ahead."

When to Use

When the teacher feels it is appropriate for the student to start sight-reading.

Inner Game

Since sight-reading is essential to all string players who perform orchestral and chamber music literature, the teacher's goal is to start developing this special technique early.

Team Tactics

Looking ahead is part of the game for all music students.

The Cellist's Tonal Palette
Mini-Game 149

Outer Game

Teacher: "In painting beautiful aural pictures, it is essential for the cellist to have a wide range of colors in his tonal palette. Let's play one isolated note and see how many beautiful hues and shades we can produce. They'll range across the spectrum from a deep purple through a vivid green to a subdued red."

When to Use

When the teacher thinks it appropriate after the student has developed a beautiful basic vibrato and a good bow arm.

Inner Game

Variety is as vital in an effective musical performance as it is in nature. Some students will react instinctively to the suggestion of various colors in the tonal palette; other will need more specific suggestions with regard to bow speed, sounding point, vibrato, etc.

Team Tactics

This analogy is applicable to all music students.

The Missing Melody
Mini-Game 150

Outer Game

The teacher asks the student to finger a difficult passage on one string while bowing it on another.

"This is an excellent way to practice occasionally. It is as though no matter how hard your left hand tries, your right hand continues to play its one-note song.

"The poor thing is concentrating so much on drawing beautiful bow strokes that it hasn't even noticed the melody is missing!"

When to Use

Anytime the student needs an alternative method of practicing a difficult passage.

Mini-Game 151, *The Dream*

Inner Game

The teacher is aware that much can be learned from even a few minutes of this type of practice. Since it is the independent actions of the string player's hands that make certain types of passages very complicated, the student attempting to play without using her ears as a guide will more easily discover her weak spots.

A simpler alternative to this practice method is the pantomiming of bowing while fingering the passage, or the reverse.

Team Tactics

All string students can play this mini-game.

The Dream
Mini-Game 151

Outer Game

Teacher: "Never forget: all good things start with a dream. Edison would never have invented the light bulb if he had not first envisioned light pouring out in the darkness! The Wright brothers would have remained on the ground if they had not dreamed of flying through the air!

"The same is true of cello playing. If you can envision yourself playing beautifully and even 'hear' the wonderful sounds coming from your cello, you will point your nose toward that target and know exactly where you are heading and why you are practicing. When you hear a more advanced cellist play beautifully, picture yourself in his place. Soon you will find that your dream has come to life and *you* will be the one playing that music with artistry!"

When to Use

Throughout the training.

Inner Game

This mini-game expresses the strong belief of the teacher and is repeated in one form or another at every opportunity. Her foremost goal is to help the student form a mental concept, both visually and aurally, and guide him in making it a reality.

Team Tactics

The Dream is for all music students.

10 Winning Offensive Plays

Offensive action never lets up. Throughout the entire game of string teaching, the experienced teacher watches for every opportunity to make positive moves toward achieving or reinforcing the achievement of her five immediate goals.

On the following pages are presented offensive plays for scoring in the game of establishing the concept of a beautiful tone, the game of establishing the habit of making tension-free motions, the game of establishing an attitude that is full of confidence and free of inhibitions, the game of learning how to study and to achieve a sense of accomplishment, and the game of helping nurture a love for music and the instrument. Although frequent references to the starting game teacher are made, most of the offensive plays may also be used advantageously with students at various levels of advancement. Most are applicable to the teaching of the violin, viola, and string bass as well as the cello.

TIPS FOR SCORING IN THE GAME OF ESTABLISHING THE CONCEPT OF A BEAUTIFUL TONE

The teacher of the starting game makes certain that his student understands that the beauty of tone produced by a freely vibrating string is the foremost goal to be sought and attained.

By programming early lessons with an emphasis on the immediate target of filling the room with big beautiful vibrations, the teacher accepts no other kind. He believes that, if a student is saturated with pleasing sounds at every session, including those she herself produces under supervision, her chances for discriminating between beautiful and ugly, or even ordinary, sounds at home will be greater. Aware that hearing oneself create rich full tones can be an enormous inspiration for which there is no substitute, he believes that the sooner the student feels a personal involvement in surrounding herself with big free vibrations the more committed she will become.

He encourages his students to listen to recordings of artists' performances and to attend concerts.

Since most students tend to imitate without discrimination, the teacher makes certain that all models are exemplary. From his viewpoint no model is better than an undesirable one.

He is an advocate of the Best Note principle, which is described below:

First, the teacher and the student together determine which note the student plays best on her own cello. Then, the student is encouraged to begin every practice session by repeating this note many times until she is satisfied with its rich resonant quality. Assuming the attitude "If I can play one note this beautifully, there's no reason

why I can't play two notes just as well, then three, and so on, until every note is a pleasure to hear," she moves to other pitches or the same pitch with different fingers or on different strings. With her sensitive ear serving as a guide, the student discovers what adjustments in her position and weight distribution are necessary in order to transfer the same feeling of balance and motion that produced the Best Note, then consciously remembers them.

The Best Note provides at all times an easily accessible reference to remind the student of the tonal qualities she is striving to achieve. Later, of course, the student will be encouraged to seek many different tone colors in order to broaden her palette, but the first step is to discover and remember how to produce a good basic tone.

Since the instrument itself plays an important role in the formation of the student's concept of a desirable tone, the teacher checks its condition and adjustment often to be sure it is capable of producing free vibrations.

The teacher insists on accurate intonation, which he considers to be the prime characteristic of every beautiful tone. Since most string students have had no previous ear training, their mental concept of pitch is continually being conditioned in either a positive or a negative way. The teacher of the starting game believes that any teacher who allows a note with faulty intonation to slip past unnoticed does his student a great disservice and that a potentially fine mental ear can be destroyed in its developmental stage by trying to adjust to its environment.

Music which has been proven to sound good when performed by beginning cellists, or new music especially composed for students by master cellists, or with their collaboration, is sought out. This music—most often written in the keys of G, D, and C major—has usually been written to bring out the best sounds of the instrument by making good use of sympathetic vibrations. The teacher of the starting game postpones assigning music which uses three or more flats because of its tendency to dull the string tone. Also, compositions requiring long, slow bow strokes are delayed, since this technique can be safely acquired after the student has established the habit of conceiving and producing big vibrant tones. The teacher recognizes that music which tends to flatter the beginner's playing is far more valuable in this crucial formative period than transcriptions of masterpieces that do not naturally complement the instrument.

In a class situation when students play individually the teacher is aware that the level of performance for each player will be higher if the pupil with the fullest and most vibrant tone plays first.

She encourages her student to participate in ensembles conducted or coached by sensitive musicians/teachers who not only select effective music of the appropriate level but also produce results of the highest musical standards. Conversely, she discourages her pupil from playing in undisciplined groups that do not produce pleasing musical results. She knows that their effect on string students in the formative stages, especially the more musical and sensitive students, can be deleterious.

Special care is taken when a student begins to use vibrato that no tension is allowed to creep in. A beautiful free vibrato must be cherished and protected throughout all plays.

The teacher of the starting game is generous with words that elicit positive responses from the students. Such phrases as "rich, red, velvety tones" and "golden round sounds" rarely fail to enhance a person's playing.

He watches for every opportunity to inspire the student's imagination to new heights, since he believes the imagination is the ultimate source of tone colors.

TIPS FOR SCORING IN THE GAME OF ESTABLISHING THE HABIT OF MAKING TENSION-FREE MOTIONS

The experienced teacher of the starting game has learned the effectiveness of initially approaching all cello techniques with big motions. She avoids small, cautious, or extremely slow motions and, from the first lesson, allows nothing to appear or feel inhibited. During her earliest teaching days she became aware that it is natural for youngsters to use large motions and that all children learn running, jumping, and skipping before handwriting and embroidering. Furthermore, she soon discovered that large motions are particularly applicable to the study of the cello because of its large size.

Great care is taken in helping the student discover the kinesthetic sensation that live energy flows *through* the fingers, not from the fingers. In order to avoid tension and rigidity in the joints, the words "press" and "grip" are sparingly used in his teaching vocabulary. Such verbs as "sink" and "cling" make good alternatives.

From the introduction of left hand technique, the teacher stresses that the weight of the left arm should be channeled through the playing finger *only*, although other fingers may contact the string lightly.

Because of the danger of tension brought about by restraint, he postpones assigning finger exercises which require anchoring down one or more fingers on a string while fingering on another.

The teacher frequently demonstrates how the fingerboard, string, or bow stick would feel if alive. He has found that execution of a technique on the student's arm is an effective means of communication, since the sensory nerves can detect what may not be visible to the eye.

Always on the lookout for any hint of muscular tension, the teacher checks and rechecks the student's shoulders, arms, hands, and especially thumbs. If tension is detected, she tries to change the pattern immediately.

She recognizes that the most common cause of tension is that the student is trying to compensate for a real or an imagined weakness. Hence, if the arm and hand alignment does not allow the freest flow of energy from the player's back, or if the trunk itself is twisted, the beginning cellist will unconsciously substitute forced energy. Thus, the teacher repeatedly checks the power lines for kinks, detours, and restrictions.

Alert for signals indicating that the student is trying too hard, thus creating tension within, the teacher knows when reassurance is needed. Perhaps he explains that a specific technique requires "getting the knack" of it and has little to do with musical talent or intelligence—for example, some people learn to bounce a ball or jump rope sooner than others.

The student's instrument is checked periodically to be sure that its bridge is not too high. Even professionals find some youngsters' instruments almost impossible to play.

The teacher of the starting game recognizes the magic of providing piano accompaniments with broken chord figures, since these seem to add oil to the player's movements. She especially seeks out music in triple simple meter to help her students gain fluid muscular coordination.

He acknowledges the merit of laughter for relieving tension at appropriate moments.

Special care is taken in teaching left hand extensions to be certain that all are made by extending the index finger backward, not by slanting the second, third, and fourth fingers forward. Also, the teacher makes certain that the fourth finger is aligned with the arm and does not jut out at an angle.

When introducing any new technique, she begins on home ground; that is, she applies it first to open strings, scales, and/or pieces the student can already perform well.

Particular care is taken when a student begins to use vibrato to be sure he does not attempt to vibrate on an unbalanced finger.

The teacher is a master at isolating techniques or problems and reducing them to their simplest forms.

Lesson assignments are planned carefully to be sure that the sequence is logical and that the music is of the appropriate level.

He considers that the orchestral music a student performs should be somewhat easier than her solo music; otherwise, she may grab for notes, a detrimental action. The teacher refuses to help a conductor take an ego trip at the expense of his young students.

She reminds herself periodically that the only sure thing about the beginning student's future is that his first string teacher will not be his last—unless, of course, he should leave the game early. Inevitably, every subsequent teacher will have her own priorities and characteristics; some will even demand radical changes. Therefore, if the student's basic approach to string playing is free of tension, he will be much better able to adapt quickly, therefore lessening the danger of his "freaking out."

TIPS FOR SCORING IN THE GAME OF ESTABLISHING AN ATTITUDE THAT IS FULL OF CONFIDENCE AND FREE OF INHIBITIONS

The teacher shows absolute confidence in her student's ability to learn the assigned material.

He exercises particular care in selecting music, making certain that it is of the appropriate level of difficulty.

By isolating each new technique and introducing it with a carefully thought out, step-by-step approach, she insures that success is not only highly probable but almost a sure thing.

When assigning specific technical exercises that could not possibly sound good, he explains to the student that, by the very act of striving to play them well, she will derive technical benefits which will help her learn to play her future repertoire.

She encourages her student to perform in an outgoing manner from the earliest lessons.

Emphasis is placed on expressing moods in even the simplest pieces. However, at no time is the young student asked to play long passages softly, since this can prove inhibiting.

The teacher makes certain that her student is well prepared before any public performance, no matter how small the audience. She also advises parents to seek her approval before scheduling a performance, since she knows that many do not comprehend the devastating effects an unsuccessful performance can have on the student.

Any situation that could possibly be embarrassing to the student, especially in the presence of his peers, is avoided.

By acknowledging to himself that even a concert artist does not have to wait until the end of a two-hour recital to hear applause, the teacher gives constant reinforcement.

TIPS FOR SCORING IN THE GAME OF LEARNING HOW TO STUDY AND TO ACHIEVE A SENSE OF ACCOMPLISHMENT

The teacher's first step toward this goal is making certain that the student and her parents understand that careful and consistent home practice is essential.

He also makes sure they realize that, while repetition is important in home practice, it is more specifically the repetition of something correctly played. The passage must have already been worked out slowly and carefully.

She encourages the parents and the student to reserve a specific time each day for practice, thereby avoiding daily decision making.

In order to eliminate one prepractice step, which surprisingly enough can act as a deterrent, the teacher suggests that the cello be left out of its bag at home and

that an unfolded music stand be close by.

Each assignment is made clear and specific, and each contains an interesting variety of music.

All new music is carefully edited by the teacher before being given to his student.

At every lesson the teacher demonstrates or explains how passages are to be practiced. From time to time, she introduces new practice techniques in order to revitalize the home study sessions.

In addition to the long-range goals, goals attainable within a reasonably short time are worked out with the student.

The teacher constantly stimulates the student's mental image of herself by such remarks as "Picture yourself as a guest soloist with a symphony orchestra. This run will sound like a string of jewels sparkling above the orchestra."

Every effort is made to help the student gain a sense of priorities so that limited practice time is proportionately well spent.

The teacher enthusiastically praises the homework when it is obviously well prepared.

From time to time the student is reminded that only a short time ago he was playing much simpler pieces or, perhaps, nothing at all!

TIPS FOR SCORING IN THE GAME OF HELPING NURTURE A LOVE FOR MUSIC AND THE INSTRUMENT

The teacher believes that each music lesson should be a happy experience, to be enjoyed by both the teacher and the student.

Knowing most young people's love for color, he chooses his clothing and his studio furnishings accordingly.

Realizing that a child's concept of time is vastly different from an adult's, she breaks up the lesson period into varied activities.

She recognizes the need for all students to play music that is emotionally satisfying and makes sure the assignments are a well-balanced mixture of pieces and exercises; she encourages the continual review and perfection of music previously studied.

Since even the most patient person can become cross when fatigued or hungry, the teacher keeps this in mind when planning his schedule.

In order to prevent the student from looking on music as some-

thing that takes her away from her friends, the teacher sets up frequent activities involving several or many young people. Often these involve students of all ages and levels, since he knows what a positive impression a student a few years older can make on a younger one.

Never is a student sent home because he has not practiced. Instead, the teacher makes valuable use of the time.

The teacher's personal interest in the student is always obvious.

She hopes to make each lesson so inspiring that the student will have more energy on his departure than on his arrival.

He strives to end each lesson in a way which makes the student eager to return.

The teacher recognizes the contagiousness of enthusiasm.

11   Signals for Defensive Plays

The string player's ears never take a break. From his first music lesson they have been trained to detect the slightest defects in sound throughout every practice session, rehearsal, and performance and to guide the player in making the necessary adjustments. On the other hand, his eyes have had it easy. Except in reading notes and watching for signals from the conductor or the other players, they have definitely played a secondary role. Though a string student is often encouraged to watch the strings, the bow, or her hands if she can do so without twisting out of position, it is a well-known fact that music can be performed successfully by a person without vision but never by one without hearing.

The eyes really go into action when teaching begins. The experienced string teacher knows that it is possible for a person to play a simple piece with a lovely pure tone, good rhythm, and excellent intonation in a position so faulty that a dead end lies ahead. A position, of course, is useless if the player will not be able to use it when playing *any* composition, including a major concerto. Thus, no matter how disciplined is the teacher's ear, it cannot replace her eye. Together they work as a team to insure the student's future advancement through the total game plan.

The teacher's eyes don't just watch the student perform—they *look* for trouble. Like the radar in an airport's control tower, their function is to scan for indications of possible problems ahead. On the following pages visible warning signals are given in three areas—the total picture, bowing, and the left arm and hand. Various other signals for defensive plays are available at the end of the chapter. Mini-games which are helpful in preventing or correcting the problems are listed. Although the questions were designed for the cello, many are easily adaptable to the other stringed instruments. Those particularly recommended for the entire string class are marked with a plus sign. Defensive action comes into play!

VISIBLE WARNING SIGNALS IN THE TOTAL PICTURE

Is the student's body slanted backward with no weight on her feet? + See Mini-Games
　9, *Jack-in-the-Box*
　8, *The Elegant Horseback Rider*
　12, *Hm-m-m*

Are the shoulders twisted? + See Mini-Games
　18, *The Puppet Dance*
　12, *Hm-m-m*
　15, *Look, No Hands!*
　22, *The Shrug*
　20, *Cock-a-Doodle-Doo!*

Is the head tilted sideways? + See Mini-Games
　21, *The Giant Floating Magnet*
　23, *The Skier*
　12, *Hm-m-m*

Is the body slumped? + See Mini-Games
　8, *The Elegant Horseback Rider*
　21, *The Giant Floating Magnet*

Are the legs sprawled out? + See Mini-Games
　11, *Cradling the Cello*
　8, *The Elegant Horseback Rider*
　9, *Jack-in-the-Box*

Are one or both shoulders elevated? + See Mini-Game
　18, *The Puppet Dance*

Does the body look tense? + See Mini-Games
　12, *Hm-m-m*
　22, *The Shrug*

Does the head bob and jerk? + See Mini-Games
　21, *The Giant Floating Magnet*
　133, *Keep a Cool Head*

Is the body leaning to the left or the right? + See Mini-Games
　19, *The Parakeet's Toy*
　12, *Hm-m-m*
　10, *Fitting the Cello*

Is the C string peg higher than the left ear? See Mini-Game
　14, *Tickle the Ear*

Does the cello almost touch the left shoulder? See Mini-Game
　13, *The Chipmunk*

Does the fingerboard look like |, not like /, when the teacher faces the player? See Mini-Games
　16, *The Rolling Ball*
　23, *The Skier*
　139, *The Magic Centerline*

Does the cello look very square, not turned at all to the right? See Mini-Game
　10, *Fitting the Cello*

Are the legs squeezing the cello? See Mini-Game
　11, *Cradling the Cello*

Is the left hand helping to hold the cello? See Mini-Game
　15, *Look, No Hands!*

Does the bow bump the legs when the student plays on either the highest or the lowest string? + See Mini-Game
　17, *Clearing the Air Corridors*

Does the cello look foreign to the player? See Mini-Game
　12, *Hm-m-m*

Is the student unable to rock sideways with his instrument? + See Mini-Game
　19, *The Parakeet's Toy*

Do the student's motions look awkward and labored? + See Mini-Game
　135, *The Virtuoso*

VISIBLE WARNING SIGNALS IN BOWING

Does the bow slip around on the string? + See Mini-Games

43, *The Groovy String*
25, *Two-Handed Bowing*
60, *The Recipe for a Big Tone*
64, *Resist Me!*
53, *The Standing Cellist*
46, *YOU Are There!*
51, *The Five-Lane Bowling Alley*

Does the bow fail to move parallel (or almost parallel) to the bridge? + See Mini-Games

32, *The Railroad Tracks*
29, *Tracing the Paths of the Bow*
51, *The Five-Lane Bowling Alley*
40, *Zip!*

Does the bow continually gravitate toward the fingerboard? + See Mini-Games

53, *The Standing Cellist*
29, *Tracing the Paths of the Bow*
43, *The Groovy String*
40, *Zip!*
51, *The Five-Lane Bowling Alley*

Is the bow stick turned away from the player like a violinist's bow stick? See Mini-Game

28, *The Bow Arm's Trusty Aide*

Does the bow tend to bounce off the string when the student plays at the tip? + Does it even seem shaky? + See Mini-Games

74, *Spread the Peanut Butter*
43, *The Groovy String*
68, *The Secret Way to Cross Strings*
31, *The Airplane Stroke*
45, *A Drop of Oil*
61, *Moon Landings*
64, *Resist Me!*
46, *YOU Are There!*
36, *The Big Full Moon*

Is the bow being drawn too slowly? + See Mini-Games

36, *The Big Full Moon*
40, *Zip!*
51, *The Five-Lane Bowling Alley*
31, *The Airplane Stroke*
41, *Watch the Vibrations!*

Does the flowing action of the bow arm appear to elude the player? + See Mini-Games

39, *The Ballet Dancer*
72, *The Flowing Scarves*
29, *Tracing the Paths of the Bow*
31, *The Airplane Stroke*
50, *The Follow-Through*
79, *Painting*

47, *The Railroad Lantern*
55, *The Dancing Bow*

Does the arm appear to remain at the same level when the student plays on two or more different strings? + See Mini-Games

35, *Comparing the Air Corridors*
29, *Tracing the Paths of the Bow*
40, *Zip!*
63, *What's My String?*
68, *The Secret Way to Cross Strings*

Is the upper arm high and awkward? + See Mini-Games

47, *The Railroad Lantern*
69, *The Gold Brick*
4, *Take a Photo, Click!*
49, *The Cushioned Elbow*
40, *Zip!*
31, *The Airplane Stroke*

Does the elbow jut out to the right when the student plays near the frog? + Or sag when she plays near the tip? + See Mini-Games

49, *The Cushioned Elbow*
29, *Tracing the Paths of the Bow*
40, *Zip!*
48, *Knock, Knock! Who's There?*
46, *YOU Are There!*

Does the forearm fail to pronate when the student plays near the tip? + See Mini-Games

74, *Spread the Peanut Butter*
45, *A Drop of Oil*
46, *YOU Are There!*
31, *The Airplane Stroke*
64, *Resist Me!*
36, *The Big Full Moon*
29, *Tracing the Paths of the Bow*
40, *Zip!*

Is there *not* a straight and direct line between the elbow and the base knuckle of his second finger when he plays near the tip? See Mini-Games

3, *The Magic Dotted Line*
48, *Knock, Knock! Who's There?*
45, *A Drop of Oil*
40, *Zip!*
30, *Around the Bend and down a Gentle Slope*
29, *Tracing the Paths of the Bow*
66, *Can You Make a T Sound?*
46, *YOU Are There!*
75, *The Hummingbird*

Do the wrist and hands fail to form a curve when the student plays near the frog? + See Mini-Games

30, *Around the Bend and down a Gentle Slope*
29, *Tracing the Paths of the Bow*
40, *Zip!*
4, *Take a Photo, Click!*
75, *The Hummingbird*

Is there a curve in her wrist when she plays at the tip of the bow? Or a hump? Or is her wrist caved in? See Mini-Games

3, *The Magic Dotted Line*
48, *Knock, Knock! Who's There?*
40, *Zip!*
30, *Around the Bend and down a Gentle Slope*
4, *Take a Photo, Click!*
29, *Tracing the Paths of the Bow*
46, *YOU Are There!*
64, *Resist Me!*
66, *Can You Make a T Sound?*

Does the power line from the student's back appear to be broken? + That is, does the energy appear to come from her hand rather than through her hand? + See Mini-Games

33, *Polishing the Furniture and Cleaning the Windows*
36, *The Big Full Moon*
55, *The Dancing Bow*
48, *Knock, Knock! Who's There?*
40, *Zip!*
46, *YOU Are There!*
31, *The Airplane Stroke*
3, *The Magic Dotted Line*
76, *What the Bow Stick Feels*
144, *The Good Water Hose*

Does the back of the hand have a different slant than the top of the bow stick? See Mini-Games

35, *Comparing the Air Corridors*
29, *Tracing the Paths of the Bow*
68, *The Secret Way to Cross Strings*
40, *Zip!*
4, *Take a Photo, Click!*
46, *YOU Are There!*
75, *The Hummingbird*

Does the line formed by the base knuckles fail to run almost parallel to the bow stick? See Mini-Games

3, *The Magic Dotted Line*
29, *Tracing the Paths of the Bow*

Are the fingers spread very far apart, perhaps even resembling claws? + Or are they so close together that they touch each other? + See Mini-Game

24, *The Dripping Wet Hand*

Does the hand slip around on the bow? + See Mini-Games

34, *The Magic Wet Glue*
44, *Honey on the Bow Stick*
76, *What the Bow Stick Feels*

Is the thumb *not* opposite the second finger? + Or does it appear tight and possibly even caved in? + See Mini-Games

27, *Pick a Ripe Red Strawberry*
38, *The Magic Tool for Picking up Objects*
80, *The Soft Rubber Bow*
34, *The Magic Wet Glue*

Do the fingers contact the stick at the second joint or even closer to the palm of the hand? + See Mini-Games

52, *A Magic Trick: Feeling through an Object*
80, *The Soft Rubber Bow*

Do the fingers look hard and tense? + See Mini-Games

44, *Honey on the Bow Stick*
80, *The Soft Rubber Bow*
29, *Tracing the Paths of the Bow*
27, *Pick a Ripe Red Strawberry*
52, *A Magic Trick: Feeling through an Object*
73, *Knee Writing*
34, *The Magic Wet Glue*
76, *What the Bow Stick Feels*
79, *Painting*

Does the little finger appear to jut out to the right rather than fall in the line formed by the hand? + Or does the index finger jut back to the left? + See Mini-Games

24, *The Dripping Wet Hand*
3, *The Magic Dotted Line*

Does the index finger hook around under the bow stick? + See Mini-Games

38, *The Magic Tool for Picking up Objects*
24, *The Dripping Wet Hand*

Does the student play in one part of the bow most of the time? + See Mini-Games

54, *Bowing on the Finger*
40, *Zip!*
31, *The Airplane Stroke*
66, *Can You Make a T Sound?*

Is the student unable to control the tip of his bow? + See Mini-Games

42, *The Sparrow Ride*
59, *Skywriting*

Are changes in the bow direction rough? + See Mini-Games

65, *The Trolley Car Ride*
72, *The Flowing Scarves*
50, *The Follow-Through*
79, *Painting*

Does the bow action fail to reflect the mood of the music? + See Mini-Game

147, *What's My Mood?*

Does the student have difficulty with spiccato bowing? + See Mini-Games

71, *A Real Bouncer—the Spiccato*
70, *The Trampoline*
26, *Finding the Balance Point*

Does the student have difficulty playing fast, separate bows? + See Mini-Games

37, *A Neat Sound Effect—the Tremolo*
61, *Moon Landings*
66, *Can You Make a T Sound?*
67, *The Rubber Bow Bumpers*
57, *Swatting Flies*

Are string crossings awkward? + See Mini-Games

35, *Comparing the Air Corridors*

68, *The Secret Way to Cross Strings*
78, *The F♯ String*

Does the sensation of the bow being pulled elude the student? + See Mini-Games

62, *Pulling through a Milkshake*
77, *The Door Spring*
30, *Around the Bend and down a Gentle Slope*
56, *Pulling an Up-Bow*
76, *What the Bow Stick Feels*
81, *Roping the Bow Arm*

Does the student have difficulty making accents or articulations? + See Mini-Games

46, *YOU Are There!*
61, *Moon Landings*
66, *Can You Make a T Sound?*

Does the bow speed lack variety? + See Mini-Game

58, *The Mental Speedometer*

Does the student have difficulty executing strokes requiring rebound actions? + See Mini-Games

67, *The Rubber Bow Bumpers*
57, *Swatting Flies*

VISIBLE WARNING SIGNALS IN THE LEFT ARM AND HAND

Is the thumb squeezing the instrument neck? + Is it tense? + See Mini-Games

110, *The Soft Elastic Thumb*
88, *The Tender Cello Neck*
93, *The Siren*
100, *Wiping the String*
Also see
  The Free Ride Approach
  The Great Fall Approach

Is the wrist caved in? + See Mini-Games

92, *Using Your Head*
87, *The Butterfly Tunnel*
82, *The Cellist's Freeway*
98, *The Arch of a Rainbow*
89, *Four Mountain Peaks*
144, *The Good Water Hose*
Also see
  The Indian War Dance Approach
  The Rapping Approach

Is the wrist arched outward? + See Mini-Games

82, *The Cellist's Freeway*
94, *The Expanding Telescope*
144, *The Good Water Hose*

Also see
  The Rapping Approach
  The Indian War Dance Approach

Does the wrist appear tense? + See Mini-Game

101, *Spring Checkup*

Does any part of the hand touch the side of the cello neck or even appear to be extremely close to it? See Mini-Games

84, *A Handful of Fruit*
87, *The Butterfly Tunnel*
94, *The Expanding Telescope*
98, *The Arch of a Rainbow*

Is the upper arm very close to the body, almost like it is hugging it? + See Mini-Games

20, *Cock-a-Doodle-Doo!*
83, *Airmail, Special Delivery*
94, *The Expanding Telescope*
90, *The Buoy*
93, *The Siren*
100, *Wiping the String*
Also see
  The Rapping Approach

Does the arm fail to align with the hand? + Does the little finger appear to jut out sideways from the arm rather than continue along the same line? + See Mini-Games
82, *The Cellist's Freeway*
94, *The Expanding Telescope*
3, *The Magic Dotted Line*
144, *The Good Water Hose*
83, *Airmail, Special Delivery*
92, *Using Your Head*
Also see
The Indian War Dance Approach
The Rapping Approach
The Great Fall Approach
The Broom Handle Approach

Does the left elbow appear to be held high and awkward? See Mini-Game
106, *Getting the Hang of It*

Does the left elbow appear to be immobile when the student crosses strings? See Mini-Games
111, *A Guessing Game*
90, *The Buoy*
117, *The Floating Elbow*

Does the left elbow appear to be jerky when string crossings are involved? See Mini-Games
117, *The Floating Elbow*
90, *The Buoy*

When the student plays in the first through fourth positions, does the line formed by his base knuckles run obliquely to the edge of the fingerboard rather than almost parallel? + See Mini-Games
87, *The Butterfly Tunnel*
94, *The Expanding Telescope*
3, *The Magic Dotted Line*
Also see
The Broom Handle Approach
The Rapping Approach

Do the fingers appear rigid and tense? + See Mini-Games
101, *Spring Checkup*
95, *The Rubber Fingerboard*
20, *Cock-a-Doodle-Doo!*
103, *Suction Fingers*
99, *Cooked Macaroni*
91, *The Committee and Its Chairperson*
86, *What the Fingerboard Feels*
84, *A Handful of Fruit*
115, *The Space Platform*
Also see
The Broom Handle Approach

Are the fingers straight rather than curved? + See Mini-Games
89, *Four Mountain Peaks*

87, *The Butterfly Tunnel*
84, *A Handful of Fruit*
96, *A Precision Diving Team*
105, *The Helicopters*
Also see
The Great Fall Approach

Does the hand roll when the student changes fingers? + See Mini-Game
126, *The Two-Hundred-Pound Man*

When an open string is played, do the fingers fail to hover over the string on which the forthcoming notes will be played? + See Mini-Games
115, *The Space Platform*
96, *A Precision Diving Team*
105, *The Helicopters*

Are the base knuckles lower than the fingerboard? + Does the hand show very little profile? + See Mini-Games
98, *The Arch of a Rainbow*
84, *A Handful of Fruit*
94, *The Expanding Telescope*
87, *The Butterfly Tunnel*
89, *Four Mountain Peaks*
102, *Four Birds on a Fence*
Also see
The Free Ride Approach
The Indian War Dance Approach
The Rapping Approach

Do the extreme tips of the fingers always contact the string? See Mini-Game
113, *Meat of the Finger*

Does there appear to be weight in a finger or fingers that do not determine the pitch? See Mini-Games
91, *The Committee and Its Chairperson*
99, *Cooked Macaroni*
86, *What the Fingerboard Feels*
126, *The Two-Hundred-Pound Man*
107, *The Zombies*
Also see
The Great Fall Approach

Do some fingers point up to the sky when not in use? + See Mini-Games
105, *The Helicopters*
115, *The Space Platform*
96, *A Precision Diving Team*
Also see
The Indian War Dance Approach

Do some fingers hide under the neck when not in use? + See Mini-Games

114, *All Fingers on Deck!*
89, *Four Mountain Peaks*

Does the hand position resemble that of a violinist? See Mini-Games
96, *A Precision Diving Team*
102, *Four Birds on a Fence*

Is the hand perfectly square? See Mini-Game
85, *The Leaning Index Finger*

When making extensions, does the player stretch her second, third, or fourth fingers forward toward the bridge rather than extend her first backward toward the nut? + See Mini-Game
116, *Stretching the Elastic Index Finger*

Do the fingers tend to be squeezed too close together? Especially the second and third fingers? See Mini-Games
104, *The Eight-Fingered Hand*
98, *The Arch of a Rainbow*

Does shifting appear awkward? + See Mini-Games
83, *Airmail, Special Delivery*
100, *Wiping the String*
93, *The Siren*
119, *Shifting Tricks*
Also see
The Free Ride Approach
The Rapping Approach

Does the shifting appear jerky in running passages? + See Mini-Game
127, *A Little Dog on a Leash*

Does the hand fall off the fingerboard occasionally when the student makes long shifts? See Mini-Games
16, *The Rolling Ball*
23, *The Skier*

Do the fingers appear to be stretching when he crosses strings? See Mini-Games
90, *The Buoy*
117, *The Floating Elbow*
63, *What's My String?*

Do the fingers appear to approach the string with a grabbing or a pushing action? + See Mini-Games
103, *Suction Fingers*
95, *The Rubber Fingerboard*
20, *Cock-a-Doodle-Doo!*
86, *What the Fingerboard Feels*
Also see
The Great Fall Approach
The Free Ride Approach

Does the student have difficulty playing fast passages? + See Mini-Games

121, *Thrilling Trills*
109, *The Red-Hot Fingerboard*
124, *The Exer-Cycle*
127, *A Little Dog on a Leash*
108, *Trapping the Flea*

Does the student have difficulty finding the correct pitches? + See Mini-Games

122, *The Blind Man's Touch*
123, *Target Practice*
112, *Fingerboard Geography*
119, *Shifting Tricks*
129, *Footprints in the Snow*
104, *The Eight-Fingered Hand*
 97, *Hitting the Bull's-eye*

Does the hand cave in when the student plays in thumb position? See Mini-Games

118, *The Thumb Rail*
120, *Amtrak Tunnel*

For plays related to vibrato, the reader should refer to chapters 12 and 13.

VARIOUS OTHER SIGNALS FOR DEFENSIVE PLAYS

Are the lessons ill prepared? + See Mini-Games

 97, *Hitting the Bull's-eye*
141, *Finger Memory*
129, *Footprints in the Snow*
151, *The Dream*
132, *The Instant Replay*
134, *The Super Sleuth*
145, *Tackling a Problem*
137, *Bridge Builders*
150, *The Missing Melody*

Does the teacher have difficulty controlling the class? + See Mini-Games

 2, *Freeze!*
 6, *A Secret Signal*
 5, *Be a Parakeet*
 7, *Skull Practice*
54, *Bowing on the Finger*
 1, *Monkey See, Monkey Do*

Are the student's responses slow? + See Mini-Games

140, *Speed Thinking*
130, *Speedier than CB*

Does the student have difficulty correcting a bad habit? + See Mini-Games

146, *Undoing the Dog-Ear*
143, *The Magic Potion*
 4, *Take a Photo, Click!*
 3, *The Magic Dotted Line*

Does the student handle her instrument roughly? + See Mini-Game

128, *Handle with Care*

Does sight-reading need improvement? + See Mini-Game

148, *Looking Ahead*

Does the student have difficulty getting into a passage? + See Mini-Game

142, *Hamburgers and Mints*

Does the student play timidly? + See Mini-Game

131, *Turning up the Volume*

Does the student's playing lack variety in tone color and moods? + See Mini-Games

149, *The Cellist's Tonal Palette*
138, *Sound Effects*
147, *What's My Mood?*

12 A Special Strategic Play—Introducing the Vibrato

The high point of the first quarter in the game of string teaching, from the vantage point of both the student and the teacher, is the introduction of vibrato. If approached with special care, sensitivity, and optimism after all conditions indicate "go," this strategic play can mark the beginning of a tremendously rewarding period to be shared by the teacher and the student. Together they witness the transformation of the straight tone so characteristic of the rookie player into the rich warm tone traditionally associated with the instrument. New tonal beauties and colors are discovered and rediscovered each day, and the playing becomes much more personalized.

At times it will seem as though an electric cord that extends from the spirit within the player to his sensitive finger pads has been plugged in and that the slightest change in his inner feelings is reflected instantly through his instrument. The tone is given life. It has a heartbeat; it even breathes.

In actuality the preparation for vibrato begins at the first lesson and continues throughout every session in the early part of the game. Each time that the teacher and the student check and recheck the positions, the alignments, and the freedom of motion they are insuring a greater probability for success in the development of a beautiful and expressive vibrato.

Since the whole concept of vibrato is based on balance and the making of tension-free motions, which are guided by the aural dream of a beautiful tone, the reader is advised to review immediate goals 1 and 2 of the starting game as described in chapter 2, the tips for achieving these goals in chapter 10, and the checkpoints for home practice at the end of chapters 6, 7, and 8.

CHECKPOINTS FOR PREVIBRATO CONDITIONS

Checkpoints for conditions which are especially important to have well established before vibrato enters the game of cello playing are listed below. Those particularly recommended for the other stringed instruments are marked with a plus sign. Mini-games useful in correcting or establishing the conditions are cited after each.

Does the student play with good intonation and have a reasonably good knowledge of fingerboard geography? + Obviously she will feel insecure about vibrating on a note if she is not sure of its exact location. See Mini-Games
97, *Hitting the Bull's-eye*
112, *Fingerboard Geography*
123, *Target Practice*
122, *The Blind Man's Touch*

Is the student able to produce big vibrant tones? + When the student first tackles vibrato, it is much easier and more natural to begin with large motions, then refine and vary them later. In fact, the reverse is extremely difficult. However, a large vibrato with a soft tone has an undesirable quality; thus, it is essential for the student to have already developed a good bowing technique so he is able to produce a loud tone that is not harsh. See Mini-Games
33, *Polishing the Furniture and Cleaning the Windows*
41, *Watch the Vibrations!*
36, *The Big Full Moon*
29, *Tracing the Paths of the Bow*
43, *The Groovy String*
62, *Pulling through a Milkshake*
35, *Comparing the Air Corridors*
52, *A Magic Trick: Feeling through an Object*
48, *Knock, Knock! Who's There?*

Is the cello positioned so the player's left elbow does not feel tight? If her arm is folded up at a sharp angle so her forearm is cramped against her upper arm, it is impossible for the student to execute the vibrato action freely. See Mini-Game
13, *The Chipmunk*

Is the left thumb free of any kind of tension? + A tight thumb can produce tension in other parts of the hand, wrist, and arm and can restrict the vibrato. Furthermore, it causes a waste of energy, which should be directed down into the fingerboard rather than up through the cello neck. See Mini-Games
100, *Wiping the String*
110, *The Soft Elastic Thumb*
88, *The Tender Cello Neck*
93, *The Siren*

Is the power line from the player's back through his left arm and hand to the fingerboard completely free and unobstructed? If the arm weight does not reach the finger pad so the string sinks easily into the fingerboard, the player will feel insecure when he starts to shake his hand in the vibrato motion. His fingers most assuredly will start to grab or push, actions which are harmful because they tighten his finger joints. The larger the motion, the more suction is required; thus, the flow of energy from the player's back must not be restricted. Since it is far more natural to begin with a big vibrato, this previbrato condition is of paramount importance. See Mini-Games
82, *The Cellist's Freeway*
92, *Using Your Head*
126, *The Two-Hundred-Pound Man*
103, *Suction Fingers*
Also see
The Indian War Dance Approach

Is every joint in the hand and arm flexible like a spring? + If not, an unpleasant nervous-sounding vibrato will result. See Mini-Game 101, *Spring Checkup*

Is the left hand positioned so its base knuckles form a line which runs almost parallel to the strings? + This is important because the shaking of the hand in the vibrato action will follow the line formed by the base knuckles. If the hand is not almost parallel to the fingerboard, the motion will be wasted and the vibrato on the fourth finger will be restricted. Caution should be taken not to overdo this point, however, because too square a hand position is awkward, makes the spacing between the second and third fingers difficult, and reduces the effectiveness of the vibrato. Even a slight shifting of the elbow backward can often improve the vibrato immensely. See Mini-Games

   3, *The Magic Dotted Line*
  87, *The Butterfly Tunnel*
 115, *The Space Platform*

Is the student able to shift smoothly up and down the fingerboard? + If not, this should be improved before introducing vibrato to help insure freedom of motion in the direction of the string. See Mini-Games

  93, *The Siren*
 100, *Wiping the String*

Does the left hand show enough profile? + If not, the vibrato motion will feel labored and sluggish. See Mini-Games

  89, *Four Mountain Peaks*
  96, *A Precision Diving Team*
 102, *Four Birds on a Fence*
 114, *All Fingers on Deck!*

NOT THE FIRST TIME

The master teacher of the starting game is keenly aware that almost all beginning string students experiment surreptitiously with vibrato at home. Certainly the more eager and precocious youngsters will not wait for an official introduction to such a fascinating device as vibrato. Although the teacher might prefer to delay this strategic play until the student has a more secure technique, usually it is far better to discuss vibrato openly with him than to pretend the situation does not exist. Almost any student who is asked by his teacher if he has tried to vibrate will look sheepish but, when a sample is requested, he will offer it quite willingly.

If, by chance, the vibrato is a beautiful one, the teacher will show her enthusiasm and will help the student guard and treasure it by encouraging him to vibrate on single isolated notes at first and to make no attempt at connecting notes until the motion is well established. If it is tight and ineffective, the teacher will explain that she would prefer that the use of vibrato be postponed until all previbrato conditions exist in good form. She further explains that in the long run the student's tone will be much more beautiful, that time and patience will pay off, and that, in a sense, when he works to improve the previbrato requirements he is working on vibrato.

BASIC CONCEPTS FOR CELLO VIBRATO

The teacher's main goal in guiding the student in this strategic play is to help her discover the following concepts concerning cello vibrato. Although these were designed for the cello, many are directly applicable to the teaching of other stringed instruments and may be used with or without modification at the teacher's discretion.

It is not a case of "the faster the better." The beginning string player who attends a symphony concert is usually overwhelmed and fascinated by the fact that professional string players are able to shake their hands so rapidly. Thus, he can easily gain the fallacious impression that speed is the goal. An extremely fast and narrow vibrato that resembles a shiver, or possibly even machine-gun fire, is very difficult to correct, and any tendency in this direction should be thwarted instantly.

The motion involves every part of the forearm and hand, working as a unit, all joints are flexible, and even the upper arm rolls slightly so the fatty tissue on the inside of it shakes.

The hand and forearm move almost parallel to the string (except in about fifth position and above) and the wrist does not twist, nor do the hand and wrist roll in an arc.

The preparatory motion is a slight pulling back of the hand and forearm toward the scroll. It is followed by an energetic swing toward the bridge, which immediately causes a rebound action.

In most cases, it is easier to vibrate with a compact hand than with an expanded one.

The hand and arm are so perfectly balanced on a single finger pad that one action causes the next and they swing just as far in one direction as the other.

The whole arm feels very loose and free, and the hanging elbow seems to float.

The vibrato has an even flow and never moves in jerks.

In the beginning stages a large and somewhat slow vibrato is more desirable on a cello than a small, fast one.

In most cases an ugly, nervous-sounding vibrato is the result of a player having an improper balance in the hand and arm; it is not because the player has a nervous temperament.

The student should be encouraged later to vary her vibrato in speed and style, but in the beginning stages the goal is to keep the sound produced by each finger identical.

The imagination of the player is the greatest motivating force in this strategic play.

The ear is the final judge in determining the true pitch and beauty of tone.

TACTICS OF THE STRING TEACHER WHEN INTRODUCING THE VIBRATO

Her attitude is one of quiet confidence; it is as though the thought of her pupil's not developing a beautiful vibrato has never crossed her mind. Even her voice has a special calmness.

An unhurried, relaxed atmosphere pervades her studio or classroom during this play.

If a student should begin to tighten his muscles or appear anxious, the teacher changes to something else, perhaps a bowing technique.

Because of his awareness that some people become very sensitive during this period of training and can develop mental blocks, he avoids any situation which could make a student feel insecure. A typical comment of reassurance is "I was actually jumping ahead of where we are supposed to be anyway—we'll come back to this at the right time."

The student is forbidden to vibrate on connecting notes in solo or ensemble music until she has demonstrated that she can vibrate effectively on isolated notes.

Any type of double stop exercise is avoided during this period.

Cello music that requires the use of many extensions in the left hand fingering is also avoided.

Though the quality of persistence is admirable, the teacher recognizes that the attitude "I'm going to do it now if it kills me!" can be quite harmful when the student is working on vibrato.

If possible, he plays flowing broken chord figures on the piano while the student vibrates on single notes, and he encourages her to react instinctively to the various harmonies.

The teacher rejoices with the student whenever a note is especially beautiful, thereby using this as a means of teaching which sounds and actions are worthy of repetition.

Care is taken not to dramatize this strategic play with an advance notice that "next week we'll learn how to vibrate." Instead, the teacher prefers to sneak into it slowly and proceed only if all signs are favorable.

Frequently, when introducing vibrato, the teacher will team up with the student in the playing of one instrument. She executes the bowing while the student concentrates on his own moving left hand, or the reverse.

With the recognition that vibrato has more to do with the personal quality of an individual string player's tone than any other single factor, he believes that it also requires the most personal teaching approach.

13

Mini-Games for Vibrato

Imagination really charges into action when vibrato comes into play! Perhaps at no other time in the game do the magical effect of words and the mental pictures they inspire have as powerful an effect on the internal workings of the player's muscles. At the same time, her entire concentration must be focused on the desired end results in sound and in motion rather than on the mechanical means of attaining them.

The fourteen mini-games for vibrato in this chapter may be used in any order the teacher believes appropriate for the individual student. All are designed for playing in the neck position. It is recommended that the reader study the preceding chapter and check all previbrato conditions before introducing any of the following mini-games to the student.

The Living Fingerboard
Mini-Game 152

Outer Game

The teacher demonstrates how the student can make a living fingerboard for silent practice by placing his right hand on his left shoulder and pulling his right elbow over as far to the left as possible. By learning to vibrate on this substitute fingerboard, the student can easily discover and establish free motions of the left hand and arm. The playing finger sinks into the flesh, and the skin of the right arm will move with the vibrating finger.

In this manner the student can practice both vibrating on each individual finger and transferring the balance from one finger to another without disturbing the swinging motion of the forearm and the slightly rolling motion of the upper arm.

When to Use

In the initial introduction of vibrato before trying it on the cello.

Inner Game

The teacher knows that this is a most successful and enjoyable method of helping the student gain the feeling of the motions used in vibrato. If these motions are well established on this living fingerboard before the student transfers them to his cello fingerboard, his chances for immediately finding a pleasing sound on at least one finger are increased.

Team Tactics

A living fingerboard can help each member of the string class. However, the right arm should be positioned as nearly as possible at the same height and angle as the fingerboard of the instrument concerned.

Jello
Mini-Game 153

Outer Game

Teacher: "Let's see if you can make your arm so relaxed that all that fat on the inside of your upper arm will shake like Jello! Hang loose!"

When to Use

1. When the student is first beginning to use vibrato.
2. Anytime the teacher thinks that this description will help loosen the arm muscles.

Inner Game

The thought of Jello is attractive to young students and serves a good purpose in a positive way. They usually think it especially funny when the teacher refers to the fat on the inside of their upper arms, because very likely it is just as imaginary as the Jello itself!

Team Tactics

This analogy can be useful in teaching some violin and viola stu-

dents as well as cello and string bass students.

The Substitution Plan
Mini-Game 154

Outer Game

Teacher: "Let's hear you vibrate on your best note with your very best finger. . . . Good! Now play the same note with another finger. Find a balance that is so perfect that you can make it sound exactly like your best note."

The teacher will continue guiding the student in substituting various fingers, always referring back to the best note.

"I'm going to close my eyes to see if I can detect whether you're repeating the note with the same finger or a new finger."

When to Use

Immediately after the student has discovered how to play one note with a beautiful vibrato.

Inner Game

The teacher believes this is the best method for developing a good vibrato on each finger. With guidance, almost every student will discover the knack of making at least one beautiful note. It is important, however, to place a rest between each note so the hand and arm will not feel rushed when the student changes balances. This part of the game of string teaching should be approached somewhat leisurely to avoid any kind of tension.

The reader may wish to refer to the Best Note principle described in chapter 10.

Team Tactics

All string instrumentalists can benefit from *The Substitution Plan*.

The Grandfather Clock
Mini-Game 155

Outer Game

The teacher stands with her right arm dangling straight down as loosely as possible.

"I'm an old grandfather clock and this is my pendulum. I haven't run for one hundred years. Start me!"

The student will reach for the dangling arm and, in most cases, will give it a very gentle swing.

"Try it again, but this time give the pendulum a good hearty shove. . . . Good! Notice how perfectly balanced it is. It almost seems to run by itself, with one swing blending into the next. Vibrato is the same way. Find a perfect balance, keep your hand and arm loose, and give a good healthy impulse at the beginning of the note!"

When to Use

Early in the introduction of vibrato.

Inner Game

This mental image of the pendulum is effective in the introduction of vibrato for several reasons. First, it helps the student understand the principle of balance. Second, it demonstrates that the size of the swing depends on the thrust of the initial action. Third, it shows the seemingly self-perpetuating nature of vibrato—one motion is a rebound of another. Finally, it visibly demonstrates that there is no stop between swings.

Team Tactics

The principle of balance demonstrated by the clock's pendulum is applicable to all stringed instruments.

The Big Art Gum Eraser
Mini-Game 156

Outer Game

Teacher: "Imagine that you have a big slice of a nice soft art gum eraser attached to your finger pad. Now erase an imaginary spot on your fingerboard. Move the eraser in the same direction as the string."

When to Use

1. When the student is first learning to use vibrato.
2. Anytime the vibrato is too narrow and fast.

Inner Game

The mental image of the art gum eraser is particularly good because it is something all students have owned and used; also, the thought of the finger pad resting on rubber helps the joints move with more flexibility.

In addition, the reference to erasing a spot on the fingerboard, instead of specifically indicating the string, has a positive effect on many students. Naturally, the string will be between the finger pad and the fingerboard.

Team Tactics

This mini-game may be adapted to the other stringed instruments by varying the size of the eraser and using the term "tip" rather than "pad" if the teacher prefers.

The Weightless Ball
Mini-Game 157

Outer Game

Teacher: "Sometimes, when I think of a cello vibrato, I envision two parallel walls about three feet apart. I see a weightless ball thrown against one wall. It immediately bounces right back to the second wall, which in turn sends it back to the first wall. I have a feeling this could go on for years and years!

"With your cello vibrato, it's fun to find such a perfect balance that you feel like you could just sit on one note and rock back and forth for the rest of your life!"

When to Use

When working with a student's vibrato.

Inner Game

The teacher's goal is to guide the student in gaining the concept that each change of direction of the vibrato should not be initiated by the player. This will help the student's vibrato assume a more natural flow and will alleviate any type of jerking action.

Team Tactics

This analogy of cyclic action may be useful in the teaching of all stringed instruments.

Shaking Dice
Mini-Game 158

Outer Game

Teacher: "Have you ever played Monopoly? Let's see you move your left hand as though you're shaking the dice. Every bone in your hand will rattle! Now try vibrating again, using this same kind of motion."

When to Use

When helping the student gain a feeling for the vibrato motion.

Inner Game

The shaking of dice is an activity outside of cello playing which describes the same type of motion most often used in vibrato. If the student has never had the opportunity to shake dice, he usually enjoys learning!

Team Tactics

This mini-game is primarily designed for cello students.

The Enthusiastic Swing
Mini-Game 159

Outer Game

The teacher asks the student to place her left hand in a high register on the fingerboard, using whichever finger she wishes to emphasize at the time.

"Keeping a good form, let your arm pull your hand back in the direction of the nut as though you are wiping the string. Notice how loose and flexible your wrist is. When you reach the specified note in a neck position, allow your forearm and hand to swing forward in the direction of the bridge. At the same moment your finger pad will sink into the fingerboard. Make it an enthusiastic swing so your hand will automatically find a beautiful balance for your vibrato."

Anytime the teacher believes this kind of approach will help loosen and free the arm so the vibrato will be more beautiful.

Inner Game

Playing this mini-game often helps establish and improve the vibrato. When wiping the string with her finger, the student will almost automatically loosen her wrist. With the enthusiastic swing forward after the finger reaches its destination, it is easier for the hand and arm to fall into perfect balance on the playing finger.

Team Tactics

The Enthusiastic Swing is primarily designed for cello and string bass students.

The Self-Winding Watch
Mini-Game 160

Outer Game

Teacher: "Imagine that you're wearing a self-winding watch on your left wrist. However, recently it hasn't been winding itself so well. Give your watch a little boost by shaking your forearm toward the bridge in a line parallel to the fingerboard!"

When to Use

When the student uses a very small, restricted vibrato and the teacher wishes to encourage him to use a larger, more generous one.

Inner Game

The goal of the teacher is to motivate the student to move his forearm with more vigor in a direction almost parallel to the fingerboard. The image of the self-winding watch helps the student focus his attention on the movement of his forearm; yet the fact that he is thinking of the imaginary watch instead of a part of his own body helps prevent any danger of self-consciousness. The rolling action of the flesh on the inside of the upper arm should still occur.

Team Tactics

This mini-game is primarily intended for cello students.

Mini-Game 161, *Walking Fingers*

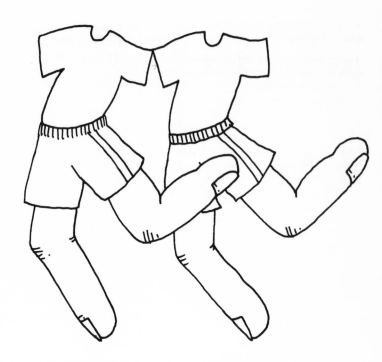

Walking Fingers
Mini-Game 161

Outer Game

Teacher: "Imagine that you are a three-hundred-pound person walking down the hall slowly. Show me how you would walk."

The teacher calls attention to the way weight is transferred from one foot to the other *before* the second foot hits the floor.

"This is how we feel when we shift our weight through the palm of the hand from one finger to another when we play slow passages with vibrato. Of course, it's an exaggeration, but thinking of this will help you get a great balance on your playing finger so you can vibrate beautifully. It probably won't even be visible to another person since your arm will be shaking the same no matter which finger you are vibrating on. Have walking fingers!

"Let's try it first by using your right arm as a living fingerboard."

When to Use

When learning to connect notes while vibrating. This should not be done until the student has developed a beautiful vibrato on all individual fingers when she plays single isolated notes. *Walking Fingers* should be preceded by Mini-Game 152, *The Living Fingerboard*.

Inner Game

Walking is a natural phenomenon experienced by all people fortunate enough to have healthy, uninjured bodies; thus, it is easy for the student to relate this to cello playing. However, caution must be taken not to rush into playing successive notes with vibrato. There is danger that the hand might tighten at this stage of development and that the vibrato could be ruined.

The teacher must be especially sensitive during this period and must change the pattern immediately if there is the slightest hint of tension. Given a little more time to establish the habit of vibrating well on single, isolated notes, the student will be better able to transfer the balance later.

Team Tactics

Walking Fingers is primarily designed for cello and string bass students.

Erasing the Blackboard
Mini-Game 162

Outer Game

Teacher: "Here's an imaginary blackboard eraser. Let's erase this invisible blackboard, using short strokes."

The teacher will call attention to the manner in which the blackboard is being erased. Almost all people will move the eraser in a series of short continuous motions which travel over the board non-stop. The hand and forearm are flexible yet work as a unit, and even the flesh inside the upper arm shakes loosely.

The teacher and the students return to their cellos and erase imaginary drawings on strings and fingerboards, moving from first to fourth position nonstop in a shaking, vibrato-type action.

When to Use

Before using vibrato on the notes at the beginning and the end of shifts from one position to another.

Inner Game

This mini-game helps the student gain the kinesthetic sense of binding together two notes which are separated by a shift. Of course, the erasing action will not continue during the shift itself except in the initial playing of this mini-game.

Unless the student is encouraged to start the shift on one of the swings, she will probably vibrate on the first note, slam on the brakes, then move to the second note. By consolidating motions, her hand and arm will be much freer and the resulting sound more graceful and liquid.

Team Tactics

Though the principles of this mini-game may be useful to violin and viola students, *Erasing the Blackboard* is primarily designed for cello and string bass students.

Velvet-Covered Buttons
Mini-Game 163

Outer Game

Teacher: "This melody will sound more beautiful if every note has a lovely vibrato. Think of it as a row of buttons. They will vary in size, but all are cushioned with rich red velvet.

"Start the phrase again, but stop on the first note that does not sound velvety. . . . Velvetize it with a beautiful vibrato. . . . Now make a sandwich out of it—that is, play the note that precedes it, then the newly velvetized note, then the one that follows it."

The student and the teacher will continue in the same manner until the entire phrase is velvety.

When to Use

Anytime the student has a good start on vibrato and can vibrate well on each finger when playing isolated notes. It should not be used in class or orchestral playing at an early stage because it is essential that the student be able to hear each sound he produces.

Inner Game

The positive effect of such words as "rich red velvet" on the musically sensitive person is well known. The teacher, of course, recognizes that later in the game the student will need to vary the size and speed of his vibrato as a means of increasing the expressiveness of his cello playing. However, the initial goal is to help the student develop a beautiful basic tone which will be the dominant characteristic of his playing, just as each person has a basic personal quality in her speaking voice even though it varies depending on the occasion and the thoughts being expressed.

Team Tactics

This analogy can be useful for teaching any string student.

Swinging Along
Mini-Game 164

Outer Game

Teacher: "All fine cellists have discovered the knack of moving from one finger to another on one of the swings of the vibrato. Let's try this. Make your right arm into a living fingerboard.

"Vibrate on the first finger freely. Now, on one of the swings, drop the second finger and release the first finger. Your forearm will just keep swinging along undisturbed, and the fat on the inside of your upper arm will continue to shake."

The teacher will guide the student in moving from the first to the third finger, first to fourth, fourth to second, etc. Later this action will be transferred to the cello.

When to Use

Whenever the teacher feels it is appropriate while working with the student on developing or improving her vibrato. It should be preceded by Mini-Game 152, *The Living Fingerboard*.

Inner Game

The teacher knows that the sensation of vibrating between notes is essential in developing a beautiful liquid tone. Every effort should be made to avoid the student's establishing the habit of stopping the vibrato between notes once she is beyond the beginning stages of learning to vibrate. The very act of bringing the vibrato to a dead halt tightens the arm and wrist, which, of course, is detrimental.

If a student has the tendency to roll or twist his wrist and hand in a rotary fashion while immobilizing his upper arm, instead of shaking his forearm and hand as a unit in a direction almost parallel to the fingerboard, he will soon discover the advantages of the latter by playing this mini-game.

It is especially useful for the student to practice in front of a mirror at this stage of his training. By sitting so the mirror reflects his left profile, he can watch his fingers swing along continuously.

Team Tactics

The principle of vibrating between notes applies to all stringed instruments.

Snapping the Rubber Band
Mini-Game 165

Outer Game

Teacher: "When using vibrato immediately after the hand has been stretched, we have a trick that reminds me of snapping a rubber band. Let's consider, for example, the first three notes of the D major scale when played on the C string. Here are the steps you will use:

"1. Vibrate beautifully on D. Balance on the pad of your first finger as though you plan to stay there for the rest of your life! Your thumb will be under the cello neck, opposite E♭; the base knuckle of your first finger will point out and slightly back as usual.

"2. Now, while continuing to hold the pad of your first finger down on the same spot, let the base knuckle of your first finger collapse in toward the cello neck. In a simultaneous motion your thumb will slide down the underside of the cello neck so it is opposite E♮. Your hand and forearm will also glide with it. While performing this motion, try to make your hand move like liquid, and let your wrist sink in ever so slightly as though you plan to look at your wristwatch.

"3. Your second finger should arrive at a spot in the air directly above E♮ at the same time your thumb reaches its destination. It's almost as though the two of them had planned to meet there! For one split second both your first and your second fingers will be sitting on the string a whole step apart. Pretend that your first finger is a stretched rubber band. Now snap it!

"4. As the imaginary rubber band folds up, your first finger will move quickly in a little arc over the fingerboard and become a buddy of your second finger. Though it won't touch the string, it will swing along close to its pal.

"5. Now drop your fourth finger on F♯ and vibrate. It's as though it never knew your hand had had an extension!"

The teacher will continue by guiding the student in the playing of the same three notes in a descending pattern. The procedure will be exactly like the motions described in Mini-Game 116, *Stretching the Elastic Index Finger*, except that, after the first finger makes the arc in the air above the big wad of chewing gum, the thumb will slide backward on the underside of the cello neck to the spot opposite E♭. At the same time the second finger will join its buddy, the first finger. The vibrato motion on the first finger should begin instantly as the second finger snaps over to its new position alongside the first above the string.

The whole forearm and hand, including the thumb, will have moved to an optimum position for playing D with the first finger as in step 1.

When to Use

After the student has learned to vibrate well on isolated notes and on successive notes in passages that do not require left hand extensions.

Inner Game

The teacher's goal is to help the student stretch her hand when necessary but, rather than holding it in an extended position, return it immediately to a more compact shape which is vital for a beautiful vibrato.

This mini-game, of course, will apply to notes found on any of the four strings in the first four positions when it is necessary to stretch the hand between two notes. The reader may wish to refer to Mini-Game 116, *Stretching the Elastic Index Finger*, and Mini-Game 125, *The Sliding Thumb*.

Team Tactics

Snapping the Rubber Band is a cello mini-game.

14 Master Tips for Improving the Game

The dedicated and open-minded musician who loves to teach will inevitably improve his game with each new experience. Since all moves and strategies in the outer game of string teaching are only manifestations of the inner game, the most significant improvements in the game stem from within the player; therefore, it is believed that true master tips can best be discovered by each person for himself. However, such points as the following can be learned from observing the winning teacher in action and consciously searching for clues which suggest the workings of his inner game.

His vision of the total game plan seems ever present and appears to influence every play.

His ability to keep priorities in line is unfailing.

The camera of his eye, when viewing a subject, seems first to use its wide-angle lens, then its zoom lens with a close-up attachment.

A childlike freshness and wonder characterize his approach to most activities and especially to learning; thus, projecting himself into the mind of a youngster is an easy matter, and guiding the student from the familiar to the unfamiliar seems effortless.

He marvels at the human body, mind, and spirit and their teamwork.

Nature being his constant source of inspiration, he consciously searches for the natural power flow; on seeing a flower, he recognizes that its radiant bloom is dependent on its stalk and roots, which typify nature's alliance of strength and flexibility.

Unafraid to speak of dreams, she believes that they are the beginning of all creative activities.

Her sense of timing is uncanny; somehow she knows when to *make* it happen and when to *let* it happen.

She understands and respects the student's innate desire to discover a concept himself, thereby gaining a greater personal identity with it.

She recognizes the preciousness of each person's life and realizes that her student's contribution to the world may be far greater than her own.

Her goal is to draw out and enhance the most noble qualities of all people.

She learns from everyone and everything.

Talent, imagination, and creativity in all people are regarded by her as the world's greatest treasures.

She loves music and life.

Thus, through the outer game of string teaching and the inner game of each teacher, whether she is helping a class of youngsters next to a noisy gymnasium or an advanced pupil preparing for a concerto appearance, the doors to human expression are opened so the music is allowed to flow out. Life is given music—and music is given life.

Mini-Game Index
by Name

Approaches

Mini-Game Index
by Number

Mini-Games for Varied Purposes

Mini-Games for Vibrato

*Approaches to Establishing
the Bow Hold*

*Approaches to Establishing
the Left Hand Position*